Here's what was said about previous editions of
WHATEVER HAPPENED TO PENNY CANDY?

"Must reading for anyone who wishes to understand the basics of our free enterprise system." —**William E. Simon**
**Former U.S. Secretary of the Treasury**

"This book is must reading for children of all ages. Its presentation of some of the fundamentals of economics is lucid, accurate, and above all highly readable." —**Michael A. Walker, Executive Director**
**The Fraser Institute, British Columbia, Canada**

"Probably the best short course in economics around and is more valuable than a college text that's ten times its length. Buy a dozen and give them to friends. This is a great book!" —**Douglas Casey, Editor**
INTERNATIONAL SPECULATOR

"Maybury's forte is explaining economics in an interesting, logical, and easy-to-understand manner—no small achievement in economics pedagogy. Equally important, the economics in WHATEVER HAPPENED TO PENNY CANDY makes such good sense. When government's economic policies make us say 'uncle,' let's hope it's 'Uncle Eric,' Maybury's letterwriter and alter ego." —**John G. Murphy, Ph.D., President**
**National Schools Committee for Economic Education, Inc.**

"There is something revolutionary about the clarity of Mr. Maybury's explanations—his insight into Germany's prosperity and the method by which it was consciously achieved has the most profound implications for our own economic policy, which is also a deliberate construct. Hurray for PENNY CANDY! A brilliant book." —**John Taylor Gatto**
Author, DUMBING US DOWN
**New York State Teacher of the Year**

"Superb introduction ... This valuable little book weaves economics, history, current events, social studies, government, math and a little science into a delightfully revealing look at the foundations and workings of our monetary system. For people of any age who think economics and the business of money is beyond them and best left to the 'experts.'"
—HOME EDUCATION MAGAZINE

"I recommend PENNY CANDY to just about everyone (children and adults)." —**Bill Cormier**
HOMESCHOOLING TODAY, Sept/Oct 2002

"This one slim volume can and should replace at least one full shelf of weighty tomes. There's really no excuse for being baffled by economic theory and economic theoreticians when you can spend an evening with this grand book and learn the ABC's of a subject about which the politicians, in particular, wish you'd stay illiterate."

**—Karl Hess, Author,** CAPITALISM FOR KIDS

"Simple, easy-to-grasp explanations of such confounding economic terms as inflation, recession, velocity, and wage-price controls; combined with some fascinating glimpses into the historical economic flubs of the Romans, Germans, British, and the Americans, add up to an entertaining and informative little gem-of-a-book suitable for children and adults."

**—Jan Fletcher, former Editor,** HOME BUSINESS ADVISOR

"The quality of the writing and information presented is exceptional, and the generous use of examples gives a useful representation of economics at work in human history." (Grades 6-12)   **—**EDUCATIONAL OASIS

"This paperback is a concise explanation of concepts and terms taught in business education and social studies courses: money and its origin, the business cycle, inflation, recession/depression, foreign currencies, and the role of government in economics ... A teacher's guide is available. This book has been endorsed by educators, authors, and government officials for its unique contribution to the education of consumers from childhood to adulthood."   **—**PTA TODAY

"An excellent introduction to economics for teens and adults that will change the way you read the paper (both the newspaper and the fine print on your dollar bills). Highly recommended."   **—Mary Pride, Author**
**BIG BOOK OF HOME LEARNING**

"Maybury's book is a valuable contribution to economic literacy. It should be required reading for every student. Buy at least two copies of WHATEVER HAPPENED TO PENNY CANDY: one for you and your family; one as a gift for a member of Congress!"   **—Jean Ross Peterson, Author**
**IT DOESN'T GROW ON TREES**

"This little gem offers adults a basic economics education which can be used in business or personal life...inflation, price controls, and fast income operations are explored with a blend of whimsy and practicality."

**—THE BOOKWATCH**

**An Uncle Eric Book**

# Whatever Happened to Penny Candy?

A fast, clear, and fun
explanation of the economics
you need for success in your career,
business, and investments

*Sixth Edition*

**by Richard J. Maybury
(Uncle Eric)**

published by
**Bluestocking Press**
www.BluestockingPress.com

# About the Uncle Eric Series

The Uncle Eric series of books is written by Richard J. Maybury for young and old alike. Using the epistolary style of writing (using letters to tell a story), Mr. Maybury plays the part of an economist writing a series of letters to his niece or nephew. Using stories and examples, he gives interesting and clear explanations of topics that are generally thought to be too difficult for anyone but experts.

Mr. Maybury warns, "beware of anyone who tells you a topic is above you or better left to experts. Many people are twice as smart as they think they are, but they've been intimidated into believing some topics are above them. You can understand almost anything if it is explained well."

The series is called UNCLE ERIC'S MODEL OF HOW THE WORLD WORKS. In the series, Mr. Maybury writes from the political, legal, and economic viewpoint of America's Founders. The books can be read in any order and have been written to stand alone. To get the most from each one, however, Mr. Maybury suggests the following order of reading:

### Uncle Eric's Model
### of How the World Works

**Uncle Eric Talks About Personal, Career, and Financial Security**

**Whatever Happened to Penny Candy?**

**Whatever Happened to Justice?**

**Are You Liberal? Conservative? or Confused?**

**Ancient Rome: How It Affects You Today**

**Evaluating Books: What Would Thomas Jefferson Think About This?**

**The Money Mystery**

**The Clipper Ship Strategy**

**The Thousand Year War in the Mideast**

**World War I: The Rest of the Story and How It Affects You Today**

**World War II: The Rest of the Story and How It Affects You Today**

**(Student study guides are available for most of the above titles.)**

# Quantity Discounts Available

The Uncle Eric books are available at special quantity discounts for bulk purchases to individuals, businesses, schools, libraries, and associations.

For terms and discount schedule, contact:

Special Sales Department
Bluestocking Press
Phone: 800-959-8586
email: CustomerService@BluestockingPress.com
web site: www.BluestockingPress.com

Specify how books are to be distributed: for classrooms, or as gifts, premiums, fund raisers—or to be resold.

## A Note to Educators

WHATEVER HAPPENED TO PENNY CANDY? is an excellent introduction to economics. It can be used in the following courses: economics, business, finance, consumer education, careers, current affairs, and history. PENNY CANDY is an excellent springboard for discussion.

Printed and bound in the United States of America.

Cover illustration by Bob O'Hara, Georgetown, CA
Cover design by Brian C. Williams, El Dorado, CA
Original text illustrations by Nancy Bixler
Edited by Jane A. Williams

Library of Congress Cataloging-in-Publication Data

Maybury, Rick.
    Whatever happened to penny candy? : a fast, clear, and fun explanation of the economics you need for success in your career, business, and investments / by Richard J. Maybury (Uncle Eric). -- 6th ed.
        p. cm. -- (An "Uncle Eric" book)
    Includes bibliographical references and index.
    ISBN-13: 978-0-942617-62-7 (alk. paper)
    ISBN-10:    0-942617-62-2 (alk. paper)
    1. Economics.    I. Title.

HB171.M46 2010
330.15 ' 7--dc22                                        2009048728

Printed by McNaughton & Gunn, Inc.
Saline, MI  USA  (January 2013)

Published by Bluestocking Press
P.O. Box 1014, Placerville, CA, 95667-1014
web site: www.BluestockingPress.com

# Acknowledgements

The need for this book became apparent when I was teaching business courses to high school students. I could not find a text that explained business cycles in language students could understand; so I wrote one. Used in the classroom while under development, it was revised over and over again until it delivered the message as quickly and clearly as possible. Many thanks to the hundreds of students who offered suggestions for improvements.

Other people read this book and offered valuable comments and encouragement about it. Foremost among them was Bettina Greaves of the Foundation for Economic Education.

Over the years, I've learned a great deal about business, finance, and economics, usually from reading books and articles. Harry Browne probably influenced me most, and others include Ludwig von Mises, Friedrich Hayek, Henry Hazlitt, and Murray Rothbard. Mr. Hazlitt's fine little book ECONOMICS IN ONE LESSON is the best economics book I've ever read.

My wife has helped in so many ways I couldn't possibly count them much less describe them.

Roberto Veitia gave me many opportunities to write and speak about economics. Bill Snavely's faith in me gave me confidence. Marshall Fritz and Barry Conner gave me enthusiasm. Karl Hess gave me optimism.

Speaking of confidence, nothing helps a writer so much as other writers, editors, and publishers recommending his work or reprinting it. Many thanks to Larry Abraham, Jim Blanchard, Doug Casey, Jim Cook, Richard Fink, John Fund,

Mike Ketcher, Al Owen, Robert Prechter, Howard Ruff, Jerry Schomp, Hans Sennholz, William Simon, Mark Skousen, Larry Spears, Diego Veitia, Chris Weber, and Chip Wood.

Additional thanks to (in alphabetical order): Michael Checken, Pat Gorman, Jim Lord, Don McAlvany, Robert Meier, Art Robinson, Rick Rule, Sue Rutsen, Franklin Sanders, and Jonathan Wright. I am sure there are others I cannot think of at the moment, and to them, my sincerest apologies; I will do my best to include you in the next edition.

# Beyond the Basics

WHATEVER HAPPENED TO PENNY CANDY is written for a multi-age audience. The core chapters 1-14 comprise "Basic Skills and Concepts."

The sections titled **"Beyond the Basics"** supplement the core material and are included for those readers who choose to tackle more challenging concepts. **"Beyond the Basics"** ideas and exercises require a more advanced reading level and a slightly stronger understanding of math than that required for "Basic Skills and Concepts."

**"Beyond the Basics"** materials appear in **bold type** in the Table of Contents and are clearly identified throughout the book.

# Contents

Acknowledgements ...................................................... 7
Beyond the Basics ..................................................... 8
Author's Disclosure .................................................. 12
Preface ................................................................. 15
Note to Reader ....................................................... 16
A Note About Economics ........................................ 17
"Smart" ................................................................. 18

1. Money:  Coins and Paper ...................................... 19
2. Tanstaafl, The Romans, and Us ............................ 22
3. Inflation .............................................................. 28
4. Dollars, Money, and Legal Tender ........................ 31
5. Revolutions, Elections, and Printing Presses ......... 39
   **Big Mac Index** ................................................ **42**
6. Wages, Prices, Spirals, and Controls .................... 43
7. Wallpaper, Wheelbarrows, and Recessions ........... 51
   Boom and Bust Cycle Since the Civil War ............ 58
8. Fast Money ......................................................... 59
   **History Repeats** .............................................. **67**
9. Getting Rich Quick ............................................. 69
10. The Boom and Bust Cycle ................................... 75
11. How Much is a Trillion? ...................................... 77
    **The Roaring '90s** ............................................. **79**
    Federal Debt Chart .............................................. 80
12. What's So Bad About the Federal Debt? ............... 82
    An Interesting Exercise ......................................... 84
    One Reason Governments Spend So Much ........... 85
13. Summary ............................................................ 87
    What Happened in 2008? ...................................... 89
    The Unknown Shakeout ........................................ 94

14. Where Do We Go From Here? .............................. 96
**15. Natural Law and Economic Prosperity** ............. **100**
  **Nations and Legal Systems** ................................. **109**

Appendix ............................................................122-154

Excerpt from THE LONG WINTER ........................................ 123
Sutter's Fort Trade Store Sign ........................................ 124
Comparison of Law Chart ............................................. 125
Distilled Wisdom ........................................................ 126
**The Truth About Inflation** ........................................ **131**
The Oil Myth ............................................................ 133
**Measures of Money Supply** ...................................... **134**
Supply of Dollars Chart ............................................... 135
**Real Wages** ....................................................... **136**
Real Wages Chart ...................................................... 137
**How to Invest in Gold and Silver** ............................ **138**
Resources ............................................................... 139
Movies and Documentaries ............................................ 141
**Internet Addresses** .............................................. **142**
**Financial Newsletters** ........................................... **144**
Bibliography and Recommended Reading ..................... 145
Glossary ................................................................ 150

Index .................................................................... 155
About Richard J. Maybury ............................................ 159
Bluestocking Press ..................................................... 160

# Study Guide Available

### A BLUESTOCKING GUIDE: ECONOMICS
by Jane A. Williams

— based on Richard J. Maybury's book —
WHATEVER HAPPENED TO PENNY CANDY?

A BLUESTOCKING GUIDE: ECONOMICS is designed to enhance a student's understanding and retention of the subject matter presented in the corresponding primer: WHATEVER HAPPENED TO PENNY CANDY?

The student study guide includes: 1) comprehension questions and answers (relating to specific chapters within the primer), 2) application questions (to guide the student in applying the concepts learned to everyday life), 3) articles that expand on the concepts presented in WHATEVER HAPPENED TO PENNY CANDY?, 4) an economic timetable, and 5) a final exam. Also included are research and essay assignments as well as thought questions to facilitate student-instructor discussion. Some suggestions for further reading and/or viewing are also listed.

Order from your favorite book supplier or direct from the publisher: Bluestocking Press (see order information on last page of this book).

**Contact Bluestocking Press about student study guides for other Uncle Eric books.**
**www.BluestockingPress.com**

# Author's Disclosure

For reasons I do not understand, writers today are supposed to be objective. Few disclose the viewpoints or opinions they use to decide what information is important and what is not, or what shall be presented or omitted.

I do not adhere to this standard and make no pretense of being objective. I am biased in favor of liberty, free markets, and international neutrality and proud of it. So I disclose my viewpoint, which you will find explained in detail in my other books.[1]

For those who have not yet read these publications, I call my viewpoint Juris Naturalism (pronounced *jur*-es *nach*-e-re-liz-em, sometimes abbreviated JN) meaning the belief in a natural law that is higher than any government's law. Here are six quotes from America's Founders that help to describe this viewpoint:

> ...all men are created equal, that they are endowed by their Creator with certain unalienable rights.
> —Declaration of Independence, 1776

> The natural rights of the colonists are these: first, a right to life; second to liberty; third to property; together with the right to support and defend them in the best manner they can.
> —Samuel Adams, 1772

---

[1] See Richard Maybury's other Uncle Eric books (see page 4), published by Bluestocking Press, phone: 800-959-8586, web site: www.BluestockingPress.com

It is strangely absurd to suppose that a million of human beings collected together are not under the same moral laws which bind each of them separately.
—Thomas Jefferson, 1816

A wise and frugal government, which shall restrain men from injuring one another, which shall leave them otherwise free to regulate their own pursuits of industry and improvement, and shall not take from the mouth of labor the bread it has earned. This is the sum of good government.
—Thomas Jefferson, 1801

Not a place on earth might be so happy as America. Her situation is remote from all the wrangling world, and she has nothing to do but to trade with them.
—Thomas Paine, 1776

The great rule of conduct for us, in regard to foreign nations, is, in extending our commercial relations, to have with them as little political connection as possible.
—George Washington, 1796

George Washington

*...All the perplexities,
confusion and distress
in America arise,
not from the defects in their
constitution or confederation,
not from want of honor or virtue,
so much as from downright
ignorance of the nature of
coin, credit and circulation...*

—John Quincy Adams, 1829

# Preface

This book is written for people who think economics, business, or money is beyond them and best left to experts.

As a technique to keep the explanations as clear and simple as possible, the book is in the form of a series of letters that might have been written by the uncle of a ninth-grade student. The student has asked about inflation and recession, and the uncle, an economist, is answering.

When possible, the letters explain by describing historical events. These cover both ancient and modern history, with special attention to the Roman Empire.

Topics include:

> money, its origin and history
> the dollar, its origin and history
> the business cycle
> inflation
> recession
> depression
> foreign currencies
> government, its economic behavior
> and others

All explanations and interpretations are according to the Austrian and Monetarist schools of economic theory. ("Austrian" because the Founders of this school of thought were from Austria, and "Monetarist" because these economists place great importance on the quantity of money circulating in the economy.)

In the 1980s, the Austrian school became quite influential. Austrian economist Alan Greenspan was made Chairman of the Federal Reserve system, although what Mr. Greenspan understood was not necessarily what he was able to do.

Nobel prizes have been awarded to Austrian economists Friedrich A. Hayek in 1974 and James M. Buchanan in 1986.

The Monetarist school, or the Chicago school, as it is sometimes called, is also gaining acceptance. Its chief spokesman is the 1976 Nobel prize winner, the late Milton Friedman.

## Note to Reader

Throughout the book, when a word that appears in the glossary is introduced or defined in the text, it is displayed in a **bold typeface**.

# A Note About Economics

Despite its reputation, economics is neither a "dismal science" nor a difficult field of study. Economics is fascinating and easy to understand, except when someone presents it in a boring or difficult way.

In order to make this book as interesting and understandable as possible, I sought the advice of dozens of students as well as business managers and investors. No concept was included until it was declared to be clear and easy to understand.

As mentioned in the preface, the book is based on Austrian and Monetarist economics. These viewpoints were chosen because good science—good physics, good biology, good chemistry, and good economics—depends upon the ability to predict.

In other words, if a physicist correctly predicts the moment at which a projectile will strike its target, or a biologist correctly predicts the effect a change in temperature will have on a population of insects, then we can say that these scientists are using good science. On the other hand, if the predictions are wrong, then the science is flawed.

Economics is subject to the same evaluation. If an economist's predictions are accurate, then his economics must be in tune with the "real world." If his predictions are in error, then his economics must be in error.

This writer believes the predictions of the Austrians and Monetarists have been the most accurate of the economic predictions available today.

Portions of this book have also appeared in other articles and books I have written.

—*Richard Maybury*

# SMART

My dad gave me one dollar bill
'Cause I'm his smartest son,
And I swapped it for two shiny quarters
'Cause two is more than one!

And then I took the quarters
And traded them to Lou
For three dimes — I guess he don't know
That three is more than two!

Just then, along came old blind Bates
And just 'cause he can't see
He gave me four nickels for my three dimes,
And four is more than three!

And I took the nickels to Hiram Coombs
Down at the seed-feed store,
And the fool gave me five pennies for them,
And five is more than four!

And then I went and showed my dad,
And he got red in the cheeks
And closed his eyes and shook his head —
Too proud of me to speak!

Shel Silverstein
from *Where the Sidewalk Ends*

# 1

# Money:  Coins and Paper

Dear Chris,

In your last letter you asked me to explain inflation and recession.  You said newspapers have been discussing these things and you don't understand what it's all about.

Don't feel alone.  Inflation and recession are things most people complain about but few understand.  They know their careers, businesses, and investments are affected profoundly every day, but they don't know exactly how. Even teachers, journalists, and politicians are often confused.  They know these things are dangerous, but they can't figure out where it all came from or where it's all going.

I'll do my best to explain as clearly as possible.  You'll not only learn some important things about your future, but you'll be able to tell others about theirs.  You will also be much better able to become successful in whatever career, **business,** or investments you choose.  And you'll be much better able to stay successful—you'll know the hazards that are out there waiting to ambush you.  As they say, forewarned is forearmed.

Before you can understand inflation and recession, you must understand money. So don't read any farther until you get a penny, nickel, dime, quarter, half-dollar, and dollar bill. Lay them in front of you and look at them carefully.

Notice the penny and nickel have no grooves on the edges like the other coins do. Those grooves are called reeding and, believe it or not, they play a part in inflation and recession.

Next, look at the edges of the reeded coins. Notice there is copper sandwiched between a nickel-zinc metal. These are called **clad coins** because the copper and nickel-zinc are clad together. Before 1965 these coins were not clad, they were made entirely of 900 **fine** silver. That's silver which is 90 percent pure. The other ten percent is some **base** (not precious) **metal** that was added to make the coin hard.

You'll notice none of your dimes, quarters, or halves are dated before 1965. That's because of inflation and recession, and I'll explain it later.

Also, something you probably didn't know is that none of the coins you are looking at are really coins. They are **tokens**. A coin is a disk of **precious metal**, like gold or silver. If the disk contains no precious metal, it is a token. However, I'll call them coins because that's what you are used to.

Now look at the dollar bill. Notice above Washington's picture it says, "Federal Reserve Note." Years ago this said "Silver Certificate," and I'll be explaining why it was changed to its present form.

Now look to the left of Washington and notice, "This note is legal tender for all debts public and private." Remember legal tender. It's important, and I'll be explaining why.

All the things you've just observed are directly connected to inflation and recession. In my next letter I'll begin explaining how. First I'll tell you about inflation, then recession.

I'll cover lots of different ideas; then I'll tie them all together in my final letters.

Uncle Eric

# 2

# Tanstaafl, the Romans, and Us

Dear Chris,

During the 1970s and early 1980s, most of western civilization, and even some eastern countries like Japan, experienced a **double-digit inflation**. Double-digit means that each year prices are rising at the rate of ten (a double-digit number) percent or more.

For instance, during a double-digit inflation, a magazine that cost you $1.00 last year would cost you $1.10 or more this year.

Inflation this serious and this widespread had not happened in the United States since this country became a nation (with the exception of the inflation of the Confederate dollar during the Civil War). However, it was almost this widespread about 20 centuries ago during the days of the Roman Empire. I'll tell you about the trouble the Romans had. You'll see there's nothing new about inflation or recession; the Romans were plagued by them, too. In fact, these were old problems when the Romans had them. The Greeks had things messed up five centuries before the Romans did.

In Rome it all started with the government. The Roman government behaved pretty much like any other government. It had **public works** projects, like road and bridge building. It had wars. And it also had welfare programs.

A **welfare program** is the practice of giving things to poor people. Modern governments also have welfare for rich people; that kind of welfare is called a **subsidy**. For instance, if you are a poor person and the government gives you food, money, medical care, or housing, that's welfare. If you are a rich person or a big corporation, and the government gives you land, money, or buildings, that's a subsidy.

Unfortunately, the Roman government had a problem. It ran up against a law of economics. A **law of economics** is like a fact of life. It's something you have to live with because you cannot change it.

The law the Romans ran into is a big one. Its slang name is **TANSTAAFL** (sounds like tans-t-awful), which means **T**here **A**in't **N**o **S**uch **T**hing **A**s **A** **F**ree **L**unch.

Tanstaafl means that nothing of value is free. Someone must pay for it, if not with money, then with time and hard work. For instance, not even air is free; people work hard and spend lots of money to keep it clean enough to breathe. Tanstaafl was a popular saying during the Great Depression, and it's becoming popular again.

The Roman government wanted tools, land, and gravel for its roads, and it had to pay for these things. It wanted horses and weapons for its soldiers to fight wars, and it had to pay for them. It wanted food and clothing for its welfare programs, and it had to pay for them, too. There ain't no such thing as a free lunch (TANSTAAFL).

The Roman government needed lots of money to buy the things it wanted. The way all governments, including the

Roman government, get the money they want is by taxing people. **Taxing** means taking money, by force if necessary, and that's what the Roman government did: tax, tax, tax, take, take, take.

People do not like being taxed—they do not want the government to take their money. They hate taxes. Everyone does. The Roman people were no exception.

The Roman government soon discovered a very unpleasant fact: when taxes get too high, people get mad enough to revolt and overthrow the government—as the colonists did during the American Revolution.

The Roman government dared not raise taxes any further, but it still needed money to pay for all the things it wanted. That was a tough problem, and most modern governments have the same problem today: how to get money without raising taxes.

There was a solution. The Roman government discovered counterfeiting. **Counterfeiting** is the making of phony money.

The usual way to counterfeit nowadays is to print phony money on a printing press. But twenty centuries ago the printing press had not yet been invented. All money was metal coins, and the government had to make phony coins. This is how it was done.

The main coin used in the Roman Empire was the **denarius**, which was 940 fine silver (94 percent silver). When the tax collectors brought the coins into the Roman government's treasury, the government would have the coins clipped. **Clipping** a coin means shaving the edges off.

The shavings from the clipped coins were used to **mint** new coins. The government would then have not only the clipped coins, but the new coins, too. It had a lot more money to buy the things it wanted.

But the Roman people were not stupid. They soon realized that some of their coins were too small and light. Some of the silver was missing. They either refused the clipped coins, or they reduced the value.

*Silver Denarius 81-96 AD Rome Domitian*

For instance, if you wanted a loaf of bread and the **price** was one denarius, the baker would either refuse to accept a clipped denarius, or he would demand two clipped coins as a substitute for one whole coin.

In later centuries, people developed an easy method for telling if a coin was clipped. They had notches cut into the edges of the coins. The coins were **reeded**. Any clipped coin was easily recognized because the reeding was gone.

As you can see on your dimes, quarters, and half-dollars, reeding is still a practice today. Base-metal coins, like your pennies and nickels, are not reeded because no one ever clips them. But precious-metal coins like dimes, quarters, and halves, which did contain silver until 1965, are reeded. Our clad coins are reeded so they will look like silver coins.

Since reeding made the clipping obvious, a new system of counterfeiting was started. When a denarius was brought into the treasury it was melted down. Some base-metal like copper was added in. The new coins were minted out of the mixture. A denarius might come into the mint being 94 percent silver and then go out being only 84 percent silver. Since less silver was used in each coin, more coins could be made, and the politicians had more money to spend.

Every year coins were melted and reminted with a little more base-metal mixed in each time. This is called **debasing** the money, and it went on for many years.

In 54 A.D. a denarius was 94 percent silver. By 218 A.D. it was down to 43 percent, and only fifty years later it was less than one percent. Look at your half-dollar. In 1964 it was ninety percent silver. Five years later it was down to forty percent. Today it contains no silver.

The Roman people knew their money was losing its silver. So whenever they got a coin with a lot of silver in it, they would save it. They would only spend low-silver coins. The high-silver coins were not used to buy things, while the low-silver coins were used a lot. Only low-silver coins circulated. High-silver coins were hoarded, hidden away.

Gresham's Law was in action. **Gresham's Law** is a law of economics that says: bad money drives good money out of **circulation** (out of use). In other words, people always save good money and buy things with bad money. They want to keep the good money and they want to get rid of the bad money.

For instance, in 1965, Gresham's Law started working in the U.S. When the debased American coins were made, people saved the old silver coins and spent the new clad coins. (The government's law says people are not allowed to reduce the value of their debased coins. If a coin says 25¢ then it must trade at 25¢ even if it's not made of silver.)

The silver coins all disappeared, and now only clad coins are used. The silver coins are all being saved by people who know that silver is more valuable than copper or nickel. You may know someone who has saved silver coins. Lots of people did and that's what caused the coin shortage of the 1960s.

Remember, the Roman government had to pay for what it bought, but it didn't want to raise taxes to get the money, so the politicians started counterfeiting.

More about the Romans in my next letter.

Uncle Eric

# 3

# Inflation

Dear Chris,

The debasement of the denarius had bad results. Each time the politicians minted more coins, they increased the number of coins in circulation. So what?

Well, have you ever heard of the **law of supply and demand**? The law of supply and demand says that when the supply of something goes up, the price per unit of that thing goes down. For instance, everybody uses pencils, but there are so many pencils that, as I write this today, they cost only about ten cents each. If there was just one pencil in the whole world, it would probably be worth a fortune.

The law of supply and demand affects money just as it affects pencils and everything else. If there is very little money, the money is very valuable, and it will buy a great deal. But if there is a lot of money, it is not so valuable, and it will buy very little.

That's what happened to the Roman money. The politicians counterfeited so much of it that it became almost worthless. In 100 A.D. a bushel of wheat cost 3 denarii. By 344 A.D. it cost two million.[2] Every time the number of

---

[2] FOR GOOD AND EVIL, by Charles Adams, Madison Books, London, 1993. page 104.

denarii rose, each individual denarius lost some of its value. That's inflation.

**Inflation** is an increase in the amount of money. Inflating (increasing) the **supply of money** causes the value of each unit of the money to go down. When the value of the money goes down you need more of it to buy what you want. Prices rise.

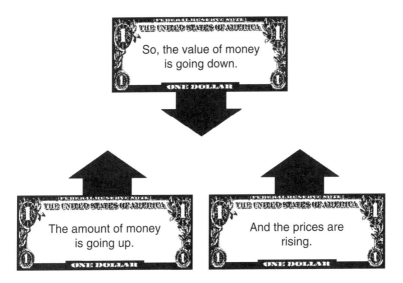

So, the value of money is going down.

The amount of money is going up.

And the prices are rising.

In the Roman Empire it was not the value of food, clothing, and other things that was going up. It was the value of the denarius that was going down. Bread didn't cost 300 denarii because the bread was so valuable, it cost 300 denarii because the denarii were almost worthless.

The same thing is happening today. It is happening not only to the dollar but to almost all money: British, Chinese, Russian, Mexican, you name it. All over the world, government officials are creating so much money that the money is losing its value. Prices are rising almost everywhere.

In 1960, there were about 140 billion dollars in the United States. Compared to today, prices were not very high. By 2009, the total number of dollars was more than 1.7 trillion, and prices were much higher.[3]

Extra money has been created because the people who run the government are using it to pay for what they buy. I'll explain this more in another letter.

It's important to remember that even during times when there is no inflation some prices rise (and others fall). But inflation causes almost all prices to rise and that's why we worry about it.

It is also important to remember that inflation is not the same thing as rising prices. Inflation *causes* rising prices. Most people get confused about this.

Also, rising prices are just one consequence of inflation. There are others, and I'll be explaining them shortly. Before I go into them, I'm going to tell you more about the dollar.

Remember, inflation is an increase in the amount of money. It causes the value of the money to fall, so prices rise.

Now you know why you can't easily buy a piece of candy for a penny the way your grandmother could when she was your age. The candy didn't go up; the penny went down.

Uncle Eric

---

[3] For current statistics see the St. Louis Federal Reserve web site, M1 money supply.

# 4

# Dollars, Money, and Legal Tender

Dear Chris,

What is a dollar? If you think one of those slips of paper in your wallet is a dollar, you've been misled.

I have on my desk a one-ounce ingot of silver. That little silver bar is a dollar. If you're surprised, don't feel alone. You are not the only person who is mistaken.

Most people think that the slip of paper in their wallet is a dollar because the slip says "One Dollar." It sounds logical, but think about it for a moment. If I printed up some slips of paper that said "One Basketball," would these slips of paper be basketballs? Of course not.

Let's see where the dollar came from.

For about 40 centuries gold has been used as money. Silver has also served the purpose for about 25 centuries. There are good reasons why people use these two metals as money.

But first, what is money?

**Money** is the most easily traded item. Of course you can trade almost anything—pencils, TV sets, baseballs, comic books, marbles—anything. But all things are not easily traded. They are either not easily moved, like a house, or their value is not easy to figure, like a diamond. Or they are not desired by many people, like limburger cheese. Or they rust or rot away too easily, like iron.

In fact, very few things are small, easy to move, widely desired, and corrosion-proof. And very few things are scarce and hard to copy. But good money must have these characteristics.

Throughout the centuries only two things have been found that make good money: gold and silver. People have tried, and are still trying, almost everything else. But they always come back to gold and silver. Nothing works better. Also, the fact that both metals have long been used as jewelry means people attach a special significance to them—they're beautiful and precious.

Some strange things have been used for money. People have tried not only paper but stones, cattle, beads, salt, fish, and even sea shells. But gold and silver are still the favorites.

However, there is a problem with gold and silver. When you use a piece of gold or silver as money, how do you know how much you have? How do you know the weight and the purity?

The invention of the coin solved the problem. Coins help a person tell how much gold or silver he has.

A real **coin** is a disk of gold or silver. It has three things stamped on it: the weight of the coin, the fineness of the metal, and the name of the mint that made the coin. The name of the mint is the **hallmark.** The hallmark tells you how good the coin is, just as the names Cadillac, Rolls Royce, and Chevrolet tell you how good a car is.

If the hallmark of a coin was Jones and you knew the Jones mint made good coins, then you would trust the weight and fineness of the coin. You would willingly take a Jones coin in trade for your goods or services.

For instance, if a baker wanted one ounce of silver for a loaf of bread, and if the Jones mint made a half-ounce coin that the baker trusted, then the price of the bread would be two Joneses.

Back during the Middle Ages there was a mint in a place called Joachimthal, in Bohemia. That's in the Czech Republic. The Joachimthal mint made a one-ounce silver coin and the coin, called a Joachimthaler, was widely accepted as a very good coin. The name Joachimthaler was eventually shortened to thaler.

The thaler was such a good coin that everyone wanted it. Thaler came to mean the same thing as one ounce of silver. Instead of saying one ounce of silver, people would say one thaler.

For instance, in **exchange** for a haircut, a barber might charge one ounce of silver, or he might charge one thaler. It was the same thing.

As you've already guessed, thaler was changed to daler, which eventually came to be dollar. In other words, dollar means one ounce of silver.

Other names of other monies also meant weights of gold or silver. The best example is the British Pound Sterling, which meant one pound of sterling (925 fine) silver. A French Franc meant one one-hundredths of an ounce of gold. The gold shekel of Babylon was a half-ounce of gold. A silver shekel was a half-ounce of silver.

Unfortunately, all money has one big problem: safety and storage. When you are not using it, where do you put it to keep it from being lost or stolen?

Another invention, the money warehouse, solved the problem. When people weren't using their gold or silver, they would store it in a money warehouse. When a person put his money into the warehouse, the warehouse owner would give him a receipt for it. The receipt might say something like, "This certifies that there is on deposit in the Smith Warehouse one hundred thalers, payable to the bearer on demand." It was a kind of IOU.

The money warehouses became banks and a **banknote** was an IOU from the bank. Anyone who had a banknote could take it to the bank and get his gold or silver. An IOU for one ounce of silver was a one dollar banknote. An IOU for one one-hundredth ounce of gold was a one franc banknote.

Until the 1960s the slips of paper in your wallet were still one dollar banknotes. They were not **Federal Reserve Notes**. They were called Silver Certificates. Any time you felt like it you could take them to the U.S. Treasury and get silver for them. The older Silver Certificates had no legal tender statement. Instead they said: "This certifies that there is on Deposit in the Treasury of the United States of America One Dollar in Silver Payable to the Bearer on Demand."

Until the 1960s, the U.S. dollar was a very good money. People all over the world wanted it because it could be exchanged for a precious metal. But that has changed. The U.S. dollar is not so popular now. The reason?

The Silver Certificates are gone. The government printed too many of them. In order to pay for the things it was buying, the government printed so many paper dollars that it didn't have enough silver or gold to back them. Now it prints only Federal Reserve Notes because they are not IOUs for anything. They are just paper, and they are being printed in large quantities.

So why aren't they worthless? What gives them value?

The legal tender statement. To understand, we must go back to the year 1270 A.D.

Back in 1270 A.D. a government that ruled much of Asia was led by Kublai Khan. Kublai Khan wanted to buy many things for his government, but he was afraid to raise taxes to get enough money.

He wanted silver and gold very badly, so he invented paper money, "paper gold," as a substitute. If he needed twenty ounces of gold to buy something, he would write "Twenty Ounces of Gold" on a slip of paper and sign his name to it.

At first people refused to accept the paper money. So Kublai Khan passed a legal tender law. Under the **legal tender law**, anyone who refused to take the paper money was punished. Kublai Khan could be a pretty mean guy and everyone was scared of him, so they accepted his paper money in trade for their goods. **Legal tender money** is sometimes called **fiat money**.

In the 1790s, the French government was doing the same thing Kublai Khan had done. It was printing phony money and backing that money with a legal tender law. If a person refused to accept the paper money in trade for his goods or services, his head was chopped off by the guillotine.

Fortunately, in the U.S. the punishment is not that bad. If someone owes you money and you refuse to take Federal Reserve Notes in payment of the debt, then the debt is cancelled. The person does not have to pay you.

However, it was not always that way. Over two hundred years ago anyone who violated the legal tender law was charged with treason and thrown in jail. That was during the Revolutionary War (1775-1783) when the government was inflating by printing the Continental dollars. The paper Continentals became worthless (although, of course, the silver and gold money kept its value), and the people did not forget it for a long time. That's part of the reason behind the first sentence of Article One, Section Ten, of the U.S. Constitution.

ARTICLE 1, SECTION 10
U.S. Constitution
*(First Paragraph Only)*

No State shall enter into any Treaty, Alliance, or Confederation; grant Letters of Marque and Reprisal; coin Money; emit Bills of Credit; *make any Thing but gold and silver Coin a Tender in Payment of Debts*; pass any Bill of Attainder, ex post facto Law, or Law impairing the Obligation of Contracts, or grant any Title of Nobility. [emphasis added]

That sentence is one of the many examples of people trying to stop history from being repeated.

If you're interested in the Revolutionary War, you might like to know what happened to George Washington at Valley Forge. Washington was angry at the local farmers and merchants because they were raising prices so high that Washington could not buy enough food and clothing for his men. According to his letters, he thought the farmers and merchants were taking unfair advantage of his situation.

At that time, Washington apparently did not know that the government was paying for the war by printing enormous amounts of Continentals. Prices were rising because the money was becoming worth less. Anyone who tried to use Continental dollars to buy something found that no one would accept his money unless he was willing to pay a lot.

On the other hand, anyone who had gold or silver, or some other noninflated money, was not bothered by rising prices. So the winter at Valley Forge would not have been so bad for Washington and his men if they'd had better money.

During the two hundred plus years since Valley Forge, the government has issued many kinds of dollars. The Continental dollar was not the only dollar destroyed by inflation. The Civil War Greenback dollar of the 1860s lost much of its value and the Confederate dollar was entirely destroyed by inflation. The Gold Certificate dollar and the Silver Certificate dollar were not destroyed by inflation, but they have been replaced by the Federal Reserve dollar, which has already been severely damaged. By 2009, according to the government's own Consumer Price Index, the Federal Reserve dollar had lost 95¢ of the value it had in 1914; it had only 5¢ left to go until worthlessness.

Until the 1930s the government allowed gold coins to circulate, and until the 1960s silver coins also circulated.

Neither was seriously damaged by inflation because, as you know, gold and silver cannot be created on a printing press.

Chris, now is a good time to let you know that economic problems are only symptoms; the cause is law. Inflation, recessions, business failures, unemployment, and poverty are caused fundamentally by corruption of America's legal system.

The legal system we have today is not the one America's Founders intended.

I can't stress strongly enough how important it is for you to understand how today's legal system affects the economy. I promise we'll talk about this in a future set of letters,[4] but first we must finish our discussion about **economics**.

*Political law is all sword and no principles.*

In my next letter I'll tell you about politics and printing presses. Remember, money is valuable because people are willing to take it in trade for their goods and services. If people will not trade for it, then it's not money.

Uncle Eric

---

[4] Uncle Eric is referring to Richard J. Maybury's book WHATEVER HAPPENED TO JUSTICE?, an Uncle Eric book, published by Bluestocking Press, phone: 800-959-8586, web site: www.BluestockingPress.com

# 5

# Revolutions, Elections, and Printing Presses

Dear Chris,

In an earlier letter I told you I'd explain more about why government inflates.

It's a fact of life that all governments inflate. They always have. There might be a few exceptions to this, but they are too small and too short-lived to be of any significance.

Both democracies and dictatorships inflate, some more than others.

Dictators inflate because they fear **revolutions**. They must not raise taxes too much or they risk being overthrown or assassinated. So instead of raising taxes, they print money. They inflate.

In a democracy like the U.S. is today, revolutions are not a problem, but elections are.

In a democracy, people who run for office get elected by promising what the people want. That's fine. However, people's wants are unlimited, so politicians are constantly promising more, and more, and more.

For instance, suppose you and I are both running for the Senate. I am trying to get enough votes to beat you, and you are trying to beat me.

I might promise the voters new schools and new highways. You reply by promising new schools, new highways, and new hospitals.

When it looks as if you might win, I offer even more. I promise not only schools, highways, and hospitals, but parks, and playgrounds, too. Since I promise more, the voters elect me.

(Keep in mind that the voters always elect the person who comes closest to offering what they want. The only way a person can get elected is to promise what the people want.)

Now I am in office and I must give the people what I promised. If I don't, I'll be a liar. The people will vote against me in the next election.

Of course I can't raise taxes enough to pay for all the things I promised. I'd make a lot of enemies and they'd vote me out of office. If I raised taxes a lot, they might even have me impeached or recalled.

So I start printing money. I start inflating.

However, modern politicians don't just run the printing presses. They use a more complex system. They use the banks and Federal Reserve. At this stage of your education you don't need to know how it works, all you need to know is that it does the same thing. It increases the amount of money, and that makes the money worth less. Prices rise.

(If you'd like to know more about how the banks and Federal Reserve are used to inflate, the clearest explanation I've ever read was in the first 100 pages of Harry Browne's 1971 best-seller HOW YOU CAN PROFIT FROM THE COMING DEVALUATION. Ask at a used bookstore or your local library.)

No matter where you go, the story is the same. In Russia, China, England, Japan, even in Switzerland, there is inflation. All governments inflate. In my next letter I'll tell you about the wage/price spiral.

Remember inflation, like taxes, is just one of the many prices we pay for a large, powerful government. It's always been that way and probably always will be.

Uncle Eric

P.S. Chris, TANSTAAFL, but few voters will face the fact that the real meaning of the cry, "I want! I want!" is "Tax me! Tax me!"

In an election, it is important to be aware of The Lie. The Lie is, I will give you what you want, and you will never need to pay for it; I will force someone else to pay for it. The candidate who can tell The Lie most convincingly is the one who wins the election.

In other words, at bottom, inflation is an ethics problem. The only way to stop the spread of inflation is to start the spread of ethics.

After traveling in 48 states and 45 countries, I have come to believe that all major problems are problems in ethics. When we begin using ethics to attack problems, we will have real, lasting solutions.

*Modern politicians don't just run the printing presses to inflate. Today they use the banks and Federal Reserve.*

# Beyond the Basics

## Big Mac Index

For tracking the decline of the dollar's value, if you are reluctant to trust the government's Consumer Price Index, take a look at *The Economist* magazine's Big Mac Index at www.economist.com.

# 6

# Wages, Prices, Spirals, and Controls

Dear Chris,

In one of your letters you asked what people mean when they talk about the wage/price spiral. You also asked about wage/price controls.

The wage/price spiral is a mistaken idea of what causes inflation. Some people think prices rise because of the following events: By joining unions and going on strike, workers get higher **wages**. Then businesses must raise the prices of their goods so they can get the money to pay the higher wages. The workers see the higher prices. They demand higher wages so they can pay the higher prices. Then the business managers must raise prices further to pay the higher wages.

For instance, the managers of an automobile company raise the prices of their cars. The workers cannot buy the higher priced cars, so they demand higher wages. The managers must then raise the prices of the cars to pay the higher wages. Around and around they go, first a strike, then a price increase, then another strike, then another price increase, and so forth. Wages and prices spiral upward.

The wage/price spiral sounds logical, but you might ask a question. Where did the money come from?

A company can *ask* any price it wants for its cars, from ten dollars to ten million dollars. But it will only get the money if the money exists. Where did the money come from?

An auto worker can *demand* any salary, from ten dollars per hour to ten million dollars per hour. But he will only get the money if the money exists. Where did the money come from?

The answer, of course, is that someone printed it.

If the supply of money had not changed, then the only way for one person to have more money would be for someone else to have less. When one worker's wages went up, another worker's wages would have to go down. When one business's prices went up, another business's prices would have to go down. The value of your money would not change.

The only way for all wages and prices to go up is for someone to print money. If the money is not being printed, then each rise in a wage or price would have to be matched by a fall in some other wage or price.

For instance, if the amount of money does not change, and the price of oil rises, then the prices of comic books, food, clothes, and other items must fall. That's because people are using more money to buy oil, so they have less money left over to buy other things (see *The Oil Myth,* in the Appendix).

Also, remember, if inflation is taking place, then the inflated money is becoming worth less. Any business or worker who doesn't demand more is crazy.

Another approach helps us understand why the wage/price spiral is a result, not a cause, of inflation. Remember your great grandfather.

When your great grandfather was a young man he was willing to work for 25¢ per hour. His new car cost only $400. In 2004, your great grandfather purchased a new car for $15,000, and workers (with jobs equivalent to your great grandfather's job when he was young) earned upwards of $10 per hour.

So why did the workers and auto companies wait until 2004 to raise wages and prices that high? Why not spiral the wages and prices up quickly and get all that money right away? Because employers and car buyers did not have the money to pay that much. They did not have the money because the money had not yet been created. The supply of money in the U.S. during your great grandfather's day was much less than in 2004.

If someone demands money faster than it is created, he simply won't get it. No one will have it to give to him. That's why workers aren't demanding ten million dollars per hour and the auto manufacturer isn't demanding ten million dollars per car. That much money doesn't exist. Yet.

But don't get the wrong impression. Some businesses try to raise prices faster than the government inflates. When that happens, many customers don't have the money to buy the businesses' products, so the businesses either go broke or bring their prices back down again. Remember, too, that price increases are not always related to inflation. Not all prices reflect inflation to the same extent or at the same time.

And unions often try to push wages up faster than the government inflates. But then the employers don't have the money to hire all the workers. Workers are either replaced by machines or their jobs are simply abolished, and the products they once made are no longer sold. If you ever go to England, Italy, or New York City where unions are strong, you'll see that happening a lot.

Of course it is possible for workers to get money a little faster than the government inflates, but they must earn it. They must produce more goods or services to sell, either by using better tools or by working harder. TANSTAAFL.

Unfortunately, most businesses, especially the big corporations, pay so many taxes that they don't have enough money left over to buy better tools for all the workers. So the only way for the workers to earn money faster than the government inflates is to work harder.

Sometimes the workers do not understand all this, and so they strike for much higher wages. Then their employer goes broke, and lots of workers lose their jobs. The bankruptcies of Chrysler and General Motors in 2009 were examples. The 20th century was a time of repeated strikes and ever higher wages in the auto industry, and in 2009 the auto industry and its workers reaped the whirlwind.

But a more common problem is the situation in the California grape fields. The workers who pick grapes allowed their union to push wages up rapidly. I guess they didn't understand that if the price of their labor goes up, the demand for their labor will go down.

One grape farmer used to hire forty workers to pick his grapes. But now the workers' wages are high enough that it is cheaper for the farmer to buy a machine to pick the grapes. So now the farmer only hires two workers. Of course, these two workers are enjoying their high wages and are grateful to their union, but the other thirty-eight have no jobs. The law of supply and demand cannot be violated.

Now let's talk about wage/price controls. Sometimes during an inflation, government will forbid people to raise wages or prices. In all the history of the world, it has never worked.

If the amount of money goes up enough, the value per unit goes down. Period. That's a fact, and no one can change it.

If the people are not allowed to increase their prices or wages during an inflation, they quit working. When the value of the money goes down and they can't get more of it to make up for the loss, they go on strike. Why should people continue making food, clothing, or anything else when the value of the money they get for their work is going down, down, down?

During wage/price controls, people stop making the food, clothing, houses, lamps, pencils, and other things they are working on. Shortages develop.

For instance, the Roman government tried wage/price controls. Food price increases were taboo. After a while, the money the farmers were getting for their crops lost much of its value because the inflation had not stopped. The farmers quit farming. There was a shortage of food. People starved to death.

When the Roman government halted the wage/price controls, the farmers went back to work and the famine ended.

Even today, people sometimes ask their government to start controlling wages and prices. The results are always the same. Shortages happen, and the tighter the controls are, the worse the shortages are.

Sometimes, if the wage/price controls last long enough, an illegal or "black" market develops. A **black market** is the buying, selling, or making of something against the wishes of the government—or above the prices the government allows.

For instance, as of 2009, the California government has not allowed some forms of gambling, so the people who gamble in these forms are taking part in the black market. In Nevada, however, gambling has been legal, so there is no black market for gambling in that state. In the 1920s, during prohibition, liquor was illegal; it became a black market product. As I write this today, it is legal and no longer part of the black market.[5] In many parts of the world, things like marijuana, guns, and pornography are black market products because they are illegal.

During wage/price controls people still must earn a living. So they often produce and trade things at prices that are illegally high; they start a black market.

For example, during 1976 in Iran it was illegal to sell a certain car for more than $4200. But the auto dealers still had to earn a living, so they sold the cars "under the counter" for $5700. They were careful not to get caught.

Also, during World War II the U.S. government paid for much of the guns and other war goods by printing money. As the new money moved from person to person, prices started rising because the money was losing its value, and the government tried to stop the rise by using price controls.

However, the politicians did not stop printing money, so the money kept losing its value. A black market developed. All kinds of things—tires, silk stockings, gasoline, oil, and many others—were bought and sold in the black market.

---

[5] There are two kinds of law: natural and made-up law. Made-up laws change often. This will be explained in greater detail in Richard J. Maybury's book WHATEVER HAPPENED TO JUSTICE?, an Uncle Eric book, published by Bluestocking Press, phone: 800-959-8586, web site: www.BluestockingPress.com

No one knows how big the black market (or underground economy) is. In 2002, the International Monetary Fund reported estimates that in rich countries such as the U.S., it averages somewhere between 14% and 16% of all goods and services bought and sold, and in poor countries, between 35% and 44%.[6]

In countries like Britain, Italy, and France, the black market is believed to be even larger. And, as taxes and controls increase, the black markets will grow because more goods and services will be traded secretly.

Despite all the things I've already described to you, some people still believe the wage/price spiral is a cause, not a result, of inflation. They believe wage/price controls are a good idea. If these people would study enough history, I am willing to bet they would discover three things that would change their minds:

1.  Large increases in the supply of money are always followed by increases in wages and prices. (Small increases in the supply of money do not always cause a change in wages or prices because other things can be more influential.) Even when there are no unions and no big industries, this is still true.

2.  Large decreases in the supply of money are always followed by a fall in wages and prices. Even when there are powerful unions and giant industries, this is still true. (Except when the unions will not allow wages to fall; then some of the workers lose their jobs

[6] International Monetary Fund web site. "Hiding in the Shadows," by Friedrich Schneider and Dominik Enste, March 2002.

because the employers cannot afford to pay them. That almost happened to me once).

3. With only a very few exceptions, there has never been a case where wages and prices rose rapidly without someone creating a lot of money.

One exception happened during the 1500s and 1600s when the Spanish conquistadors were stealing the Aztecs' and Incas' gold and silver. The conquistadors stole so much gold and silver and sent so much back to Europe that the **money supply** in Europe rose quite a bit. So wages and prices rose in Europe. When the Aztecs and Incas ran out of gold and silver, European wages and prices leveled off. The gold discoveries in California and Australia (1848+) and in Alaska (1896-1902) were also inflations that affected prices.

I guess even today the same thing could happen if enough money was moved from one part of the world to another. But I don't know of any such case except a few small incidents in Switzerland. Sometimes there will be a war or some other trouble somewhere and people will move a lot of their money into Switzerland. The Swiss are occasionally bothered by that, but not like the Europeans were 400 years ago.

Remember the wage/price spiral is a result, not a cause, of inflation. The general, over-all level of wages and prices cannot rise unless someone creates more money. Wage/price controls have never worked because they could not stop the money supply from increasing.

Next I'll tell you about runaway inflation.

Uncle Eric

# 7

# Wallpaper, Wheelbarrows, and Recessions

Dear Chris,

By now you're probably saying, "But the world's governments cannot keep creating money forever. They must stop sometime. Prices can't rise forever!"

Let's look again at history. Inflation isn't an unusual event. In fact, it's quite common. I'd say it happens about as often as major wars, earthquakes, and other troubles.

When an inflation gets bad enough for prices to be rising rapidly, every few hours, it's called a **runaway inflation**. On the next page is a partial list of runaway inflations.

Keep in mind that these are not just double-digit inflations, they are runaway inflations. Much worse.

For instance, in Germany a pound of butter cost 1.4 marks in 1914. By 1918 the price was up to 3.0 marks. Four years later it was 2400 marks, and the next year it was 6,000,000,000,000 (six trillion!) marks. In 1914 one egg cost less than one mark. Nine years later an egg was 80,000,000,000 (eighty billion marks).

# A Partial List of Runaway Inflations

| Nation | Year |
|---|---|
| America | 1781 |
| America | 1865 |
| Angola | 1994 |
| Argentina | 1991 |
| Austria | 1922 |
| Belarus | 2000 |
| Bolivia | 1985 |
| Bosnia | 1993 |
| Brazil | 1971 |
| Brazil | 1994 |
| Bulgaria | 1997 |
| Chile | 1973 |
| China | 1947 to 1955 |
| France | 1796 |
| France | 1940s |
| Georgia | 1995 |
| Germany | 1923 |
| Germany | 1940s |
| Greece | 1944 |
| Hungary | 1946 |
| Indonesia | 1965 |
| Indonesia | 1998 |
| Israel | 1984 |
| Japan | 1940s |
| Mexico | 1980s |
| Mozambique | 2004 |
| Nicaragua | 1980s |
| Peru | 1991 |
| Poland | 1990s |
| Romania | 2005 |
| Russia | 1924 |
| Russia | 1990s |
| Turkey | 2005 |
| Ukraine | 1995 |
| Yugoslavia | 1990 |
| Zaire | 1990s |
| Zimbabwe | 2009 |

In the Hungarian inflation of 1946, the money lost all its value. You could wallpaper a room more cheaply with money than with wallpaper. It took so much money to buy things that people had to carry their cash in wheelbarrows.

Sometimes governments will even try to use runaway inflation as a weapon of war. During World War II the German government counterfeited millions of British pounds, and rumor has it that the British and American governments were printing German marks, and the Russians were printing U.S. money.

But runaway inflations usually happen because, once started, an inflation is hard to stop. To see why, let's look at an easy example. I'll make up a story. To keep things simple, I'll talk only about your home town, and I'll assume the inflating is done by a counterfeiter rather than a government.

Pretend you are the owner of a music shop in your home town, and I am your friendly local counterfeiter. I begin printing money to pay my bills, just as government does, and I am generous enough to share it with my friends, just like the government.

My friends change their spending habits. So long as producers and/or outsiders continue to supply more products, my friends are no longer satisfied buying hamburgers and economy cars. Instead, they buy steaks and luxury cars. They also use their extra money to buy lots of music.

Shortly after I begin printing money, you notice the demand for music has gone way up. Being a wise merchant, you take advantage of the opportunity. You expand your business. You buy plenty of music. You hire more clerks. You buy a larger building.

Everyone is happy—until prices start rising. Being a concerned citizen, I am upset over the fact that my inflation is destroying the value of my friends' money. I stop printing money. By this time, too, the suppliers are balking at accepting any more paper money.

Suddenly the demand for music goes back down. Fewer people are buying music. Your extra clerks have no work to do, so you must lay them off. You have too much music, so you must sell your extra inventory at a loss. You must sell your large store and move back to the small one, and the move back to the small store costs you much time and money.

Unemployment rises while the clerks retrain and look for other jobs. You are losing money. A depression has hit your home town.

In other words, my inflation caused you to make mistakes. You hired too many people. You unwisely spent your money on a new store and extra music.

Correcting your mistakes meant laying off your employees. You were losing money. A depression happened.

A **depression** is the correction period following an inflation. During a depression, businesses go broke and people lose their jobs. Many become poorer. It's all caused by the inflation.

Sometimes governments stop inflating, but then they get worried about the depression. They see people out of work, so they start inflating again. This stops the depression for a while.

When a government stops a depression before it is fully under way, that's a recession. A **recession** is the beginning of a depression that never went all the way.

That's why we have inflation, then recession, then inflation, then recession, and so on. Politicians inflate until they get scared of rising prices. Then they stop inflating until they get scared of the unemployment. Then they start inflating again. This up, down, up, down motion is called the **business cycle**.

(Chris, I will thoroughly explain the business cycle to you in a future set of letters.[7])

Each round of inflation causes businesspeople to make more mistakes. More corrections are needed. So each correction needs to be worse than the last.

Therefore, each recession needs a little more inflation to stop it, so each inflation must be a little worse than the last.

The severity of a recession depends on how much inflation is slowed. For instance, the 1975 recession was very bad because the inflation had been slowed a lot. Very little money was being created. But the 1970 recession was very mild because inflation slowed very little. The 1982 recession was terrible.

---

[7] Uncle Eric is referring to Richard J. Maybury's book THE CLIPPER SHIP STRATEGY, an Uncle Eric book, published by Bluestocking Press, phone: 800-959-8586, web site: www.BluestockingPress.com

How do you tell the difference between a depression and a recession? An old joke says that if your neighbor loses his job, that's a recession; if you lose your lob, it's a depression.

Really though, it's easy to tell the difference. If the inflation is slowed down or stopped for a few months, it's a recession. If the inflation stops for years, it's a depression. Inflation must be stopped permanently if the economy is to recover on a sound, long-term basis.

In fact, depressions usually involve deflations. A **deflation** is when the amount of money goes down, which causes the value of the money to go up. Prices fall.

For now, remember that recessions or depressions are due to the bad policy of inflation. They reveal the mistakes and malinvestments businesses made under the influence of the inflation. Thus recessions or depressions are periods of correction in which business people try to better adjust production and prices to what consumers want.

Even though it appears government is rescuing the economy when it resorts to inflation once more, and brings a recession or depression to an end, it is actually only postponing the end to inflation. It is storing up still more distortion and **malinvestment** for the future and making a return to sound money still more difficult.

Many years ago no one understood the business cycle. No one knew what caused it, and some people made all kinds of silly suggestions. For instance, some people thought the business cycle was caused by sunspots.

But today we know the business cycle is caused by the amount of money being shifted up and down.

It's important to remember that the politicians would like to stop inflating. They hate rising prices just as we do. But they have been inflating for many decades, and if they stop, a depression will happen. Once in a while they do slow the inflation or stop it temporarily. This causes a recession, like in 1970, 1975, 1982, 1990, and 2001. But they are afraid to stop inflation altogether. If I were one of them, I would be, too.

The economy is now so disorganized that the number of dollars officials print to forestall depression is probably greater than the number they print to finance their spending.

Chris, here is an example (a real case of people making bad decisions—decisions that had to be corrected because of too much money being freely available):

Many people in Atlanta, Georgia, had made bad real estate investments during the early 1970s when the government was creating a lot of money. Even a few bankers were caught up in the get-rich-quick fever.

Then, in 1974, when the government stopped inflating, all these bad investments came to light. Many people were very sorry they hadn't been more careful. Some large companies went broke.

As the people in Atlanta discovered, inflation is like being hooked on heroin. Once you've gotten into it, you can only stop by going through the **withdrawals**, the depression.

How bad do the withdrawals need to be? I'll tell you later.

Until then, remember that inflation causes recessions and depressions. The only way to never have recessions and depressions is to never inflate.

Also, remember that inflation is like taxes. It's just one of the prices we pay for a big government.

Uncle Eric

# Boom and Bust Cycle since the Civil War*

| Peak of Boom | Bottom of Bust | Duration (Months) Bust | Boom |
|---|---|---|---|
| April 1865 | December 1867 | 32 | 18 |
| June 1869 | December 1870 | 18 | 34 |
| October 1873 | March 1879 | 65 | 36 |
| March 1882 | May 1885 | 38 | 22 |
| March 1887 | April 1888 | 13 | 27 |
| July 1890 | May 1891 | 10 | 20 |
| January 1893 | June 1894 | 17 | 18 |
| December 1895 | June 1897 | 18 | 24 |
| June 1899 | December 1900 | 18 | 21 |
| September 1902 | August 1904 | 23 | 33 |
| May 1907 | June 1908 | 13 | 19 |
| January 1910 | January 1912 | 24 | 12 |
| January 1913 | December 1914 | 23 | 44 |
| August 1918 | March 1919 | 7 | 10 |
| January 1920 | July 1921 | 18 | 22 |
| May 1923 | July 1924 | 14 | 27 |
| October 1926 | November 1927 | 13 | 21 |
| August 1929 | March 1933 | 43 | 50 |
| May 1937 | June 1938 | 13 | 80 |
| February 1945 | October 1945 | 8 | 37 |
| November 1948 | October 1949 | 11 | 45 |
| July 1953 | May 1954 | 10 | 39 |
| August 1957 | April 1958 | 8 | 24 |
| April 1960 | February 1961 | 10 | 106 |
| December 1969 | November 1970 | 11 | 36 |
| November 1973 | March 1975 | 16 | 58 |
| January 1980 | July 1980 | 6 | 12 |
| July 1981 | November 1982 | 16 | 92 |
| July 1990 | March 1991 | 9 | 109 |
| March 2001 | November 2001 | 8 | 74 |

| *so far, as of March 2009 | **Average length of busts:** 18 | |
|---|---|---|
| | **Average length of booms:** | **39** |

Most of the inflation of the 1800s was by small private banks that issued their own currencies and then inflated it. These were called wildcat banks. In 1913, the small private wildcat banks were brought under control of the giant Federal Reserve System which then began inflating. The Federal Reserve has been called the world's largest wildcat bank.

# 8

# Fast Money

Dear Chris,

One aspect of inflation which is poorly understood by almost everyone, including some economists, is velocity. In the mid-1980s, officials became very concerned about it. Economists in the Federal Reserve discuss it frequently. Some are also discussing a related topic called the demand for money.

First, I'll say a few words about velocity, then the **demand for money**.

Like everything else about economics, velocity is easy to understand if you ignore all the complex theory. Simply think about people. Just keep thinking about the way individual human beings behave.

Many years ago when I was still a student, I asked an **economist** to tell me about velocity. He said, "Velocity is the component of the Equation of Exchange which is computed by dividing PQ by $M_1$." I'll try to be a bit clearer than that.

The economist meant to say that **velocity** is the speed at which money changes hands. For instance, if a dollar bill is traded once in a year, its velocity is one. If that dollar changes hands five times in a year, then its velocity is five.

Imagine ten people sitting in a circle. Each has two things in his hands, a dollar bill and a baseball card. Now imagine each person selling his card to the person on his right for one dollar. Every card has been sold, and every dollar has changed hands once. The velocity of the money is one.

Now imagine the same circle of ten people. Each has a baseball card, but only one person has a dollar. Now imagine the person with the dollar buying his neighbor's card. The neighbor then uses the dollar to buy his neighbor's card. That neighbor uses the dollar to buy his neighbor's card, and so forth. The dollar goes all the way around the circle, each person using it to buy a card.

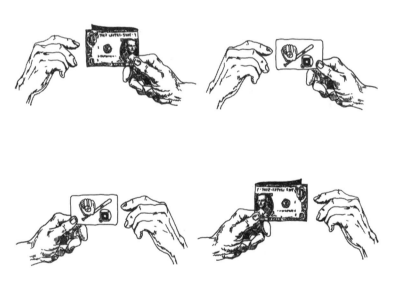

That single dollar has done the same work as the ten dollars in the first example. All the cards were sold for one dollar. But, the money changed hands not once but ten times. Velocity was ten.

In other words, a small amount of money can do the same work as a large amount. It can be used in the same number of transactions and have the same effect on prices if it changes hands quickly enough.

Why would people trade their money away faster? What would make you trade your money away faster?

A decline in the demand for money. When I said in an earlier letter that money responds to the law of supply and demand, I meant exactly that. There is a demand for money as well as a supply of it. After all, you want money, right? Most people do.

When demand for the dollar falls, this means people are more willing to spend dollars than to hold them. They buy more goods and services and keep fewer dollars. This has the same effect on prices as an increase in the money supply. People are spending faster, so each dollar is used in more transactions and has more effect on prices.

If demand for the dollar rises, people are more willing to hold dollars and less willing to spend them. Their buying decreases and this has the same effect as a decrease in the money supply. The dollars exist but they aren't being used as much, and they aren't affecting prices as much.

A very important point here is that the demand for money is the cause, and velocity is the effect. If the demand for money falls, the money changes hands faster—the "velocity of circulation" rises; if the demand for money rises, velocity falls.

Some people speak as if velocity were a force in itself, but it's not, it's a *symptom*. When we want to know if the demand for the dollar is rising or falling, we can look at how fast the dollar is changing hands.

Inflation usually goes in three stages. Each stage is caused by a change in the demand for money. Here are three examples:

1. Suppose you earn twenty dollars and you want to buy a radio. Last year the radio cost $10.00, but the government has been printing money so the radio has risen to $12.00. You decide to hang onto your money hoping the radio will come back down to $10.00.

   In this first example, you did not spend your money. You held onto your dollars, so they did not circulate. Your demand for dollars was high and the velocity of your dollars was low.

   In the first stages of inflation, people save their money, waiting for prices to fall. Because they hold onto their money it doesn't enter the market to bid up prices. Little of the newly printed money is being spent and prices cannot rise very fast.

2. Suppose you still have your twenty dollars, and officials are still printing money. The price of the radio is up to $15.00, and you decide to buy now before the price goes higher. Your brother, who intended to buy a radio next year, also decides to buy now before the price goes higher.

   Notice, your brother has speeded up his buying. He is getting rid of his money faster than he intended to. The money is circulating faster. Demand for dollars has fallen and velocity has increased.

In the second stage of inflation, the money changes hands faster. A little bit of money is beginning to do the work of a lot of money. Prices start rising faster than the money is being printed.

3. Suppose you earn another twenty dollars. The price of the radio has risen to $20.00. You do not want another radio but your money is losing its value. You know radios are not losing their value. You trade your money for another radio because you trust the value of radios more than you trust the value of dollars. Your friends and neighbors are doing the same thing. They are buying anything they can find just so they can get rid of their money before it becomes worthless.

In the third stage of inflation, the money changes hands very fast. People don't want it and they're trying to get rid of it. The demand for money is falling like a stone and velocity is skyrocketing.

In the third stage, no one can stop the money from losing its value. Even if the printing presses are stopped, the money becomes worthless because no one wants it.

The third stage is the final, runaway stage of inflation. It is ended when people completely reject the money and begin using something new for money. They usually switch over to a good foreign **currency** or to gold or silver. During American runaway inflations, they generally switch over to gold or silver.

If you ever spend time in a Latin American country, you might get a chance to see inflation go through all three stages. It's very common in places like Brazil, Argentina, and Peru. For instance, it happened in Chile during the mid-1970s.

In some parts of the world, the inflation is usually stopped during the second stage. A depression or recession follows immediately. But in the Latin American countries, the inflations often go all the way before the corrections are allowed to begin.

Now that you know about velocity, you may be a little worried about it. You may be wondering what keeps velocity from suddenly going wild and destroying the money. What keeps velocity under control?

The answer is that the people, you and I and everyone else, keep velocity under control. In fact, there is probably no other part of the economy that is as democratically controlled as velocity.

Every person makes daily decisions about spending his money. Therefore, although he may not realize it, every person makes daily decisions about velocity. If a person spends his money more quickly than usual, velocity increases; if he spends his money more slowly than usual, velocity falls.

Actually though, people do not change their spending habits very much unless they have a good reason, so velocity seldom varies except gradually over years or decades. However, two things can cause people to change their spending habits enough to change velocity quickly. Either (1) someone tampers with the supply of money, or (2) the government, which prints the money and enforces the legal tender laws, begins to go out of business.

A good example of #1 happened in the U.S. between 1915 and 1929. During World War I and the 1920s, the government caused a big increase in the supply of money. Those newly created dollars were the main thing that caused the "Roaring Twenties" to roar. The inflation caused stock prices to skyrocket, so millions of people felt rich, temporarily. Few people realized that the inflation that had made them feel so prosperous was setting the stage for the Great Depression.

The inflation caused people to spend their money faster, so during the 1920s, velocity rose. Then during the early 1930s, the Depression era, the government stopped expanding the money supply and prices fell. People were fearful about losing their jobs, so they avoided spending money, and velocity fell, too.

A good example of #2 happened in Vietnam during the 1970s. When the North Vietnamese army invaded South Vietnam, everyone knew that the South Vietnamese government would soon be out of business. The South Vietnamese people realized that no one would be enforcing the legal tender laws.

The Vietnamese money was called the piaster. Demand for it plunged. The Vietnamese began spending their piasters as quickly as possible, and the velocity of the money rose violently.

Prices went wild and people tried to trade their piasters for anything. They preferred gold, and some of them fled to the U.S. carrying lots of the yellow metal, but they would take almost anything they could get. It was not unusual for the American airmen who were flying into Vietnam to be offered large bundles of piasters in exchange for a few U.S. dollars.

A final point. The fact that inflations go through three stages does not mean they go through these stages in an inevitable, mechanical way. They can go from stage one to stage two then back to stage one again if the government is willing to trigger a recession.

For instance, in the late 1970s, the U.S. was in stage two and moving toward stage three. The government tightened the money supply, thereby giving us the back-to-back 1980 and 1982 recessions. The '82 recession was the worst since the Great Depression of the 1930s. The demand for money stabilized and velocity stopped climbing. In fact, statistics show velocity began falling. Apparently we went back into stage one.

The 1980s were the first time since World War II that velocity had fallen. Government economists became quite concerned about it. Many shifted their attention away from the supply of money to the demand for money.

Chris, I'll discuss velocity and the demand for money in greater depth in a future set of letters.[8] For now remember, inflation goes through three stages and these stages are caused by changes in the demand for money. Velocity is a way to know how the demand for money is changing.

Uncle Eric

---

[8] To learn more about velocity and the demand for money, read Richard J. Maybury's book THE MONEY MYSTERY, an Uncle Eric book, published by Bluestocking Press, web site: www.BluestockingPress.com, phone: 800-959-8586.

# Beyond the Basics

## History Repeats

In the inflation of World War I and the 1920s, the U.S. money supply rose from $16.39 billion in 1914 to $46.6 billion in 1929.[9]  Yet, prices of most raw materials and consumer goods rose little or not at all.  The government's **Consumer Price Index** was at 60 in 1920, and at 51 in 1929.  These falling prices led some people to think inflation had been conquered.

Actually, these prices did not rise because the excess money was not spent on raw materials or consumer goods, but on stocks.  In 1920 stocks were at 75; in 1929 they hit 381,[10] for a rise of 408% during the so-called Roaring '20s.  Stock investors felt wonderfully rich.  They went on spending sprees and thought the boom would last forever.

The 1990s were a repeat of the 1920s.  In the Roaring '90s, many people thought inflation had been conquered because prices of raw materials and consumer goods rose very little.  Despite the money supply rising from $2.3 trillion in 1990 to $4.2 trillion in 1999[11] —83%—there were many news stories about

---

[9] Using the M1 measure of money supply which was the most accurate measure at that time.

[10] Dow Jones Industrial Average.

[11] Using the new MZM measure of money supply. (See page 134 for an explanation of MZM.)

"The End Of Inflation!" The Consumer Price Index in the Roaring '90s was rising at only two to three percent per year, much less than the double-digit rates of the early 1980s.

Inflation did not end in the Roaring '90s, the money was spent on stocks as in the Roaring '20s. In 1990 the Dow Jones Industrial Average was 2,500; in 1999 it hit 11,000. Stock investors felt wonderfully rich and went on spending sprees thinking the boom would last forever.

Do you remember what happened in 1929 when inflation of the money supply was halted?

The Great 1929 Stock Market Crash.

Stocks lost nine tenths of their value and took 25 years to return to their 1929 level.

By the end of the Roaring '20s, many people who knew little about economic history were deeply into stocks. When multimillionaire Joseph Kennedy (father of President John F. Kennedy) was given a stock tip by a shoeshine boy, he sold all his stocks just weeks before the great crash.

Financier Bernard Baruch explained, "When beggars and shoeshine boys, barbers and beauticians can tell you how to get rich, it is time to remind yourself that there is no more dangerous illusion than the belief that one can get something for nothing."

By 2001, the great stock market boom of the 1990s was over, and stocks crashed in a nearly identical replay of 1929. The crash was followed by the 2001 recession, which was quickly ended by a huge new burst of money creation. Much of this money then went into real estate and raw materials.

# 9

# Getting Rich Quick

Dear Chris,

One of the strangest and most dangerous things about inflation is that it is usually accompanied by fast-action, get-rich-quick fads. The reason isn't hard to understand if we look at an example.

Suppose you live in an area where some powerful politician has gotten elected by promising to build a big new military weapons plant. (The politician won the election because his opponent only promised to build a small weapons plant.)

The new plant is being built, and the government has decided to pay for it by printing money. You leave your $10,000 per year job and take one of the $20,000 jobs at the new plant. So you are receiving thousands of dollars of the newly created money—that's your reward for voting for the politician.

Now that your income has risen, you decide to invest $5000 somewhere. You look around for a good investment and discover there is a shortage of apartments in nearby Destitutionville. Rents and land prices are rising in that area (remember the law of supply and demand) so you decide to get in on a good thing. You become an apartment owner.

You have many neighbors who are also benefiting from the new weapons plant, and they start buying property in Destitutionville, too. Soon real estate prices in Destitutionville are skyrocketing. Things turned out even better than you expected. Your $5,000 has become $50,000.

The real estate buyers who are now arriving in Destitutionville are finding there is no property left to buy. No one will sell because everyone expects prices to keep rising.

The new buyers start building their own apartments. Soon the apartment shortage turns into a surplus. A few pessimists point out that there is no longer any good reason for prices to keep rising, but no one ever listens to a party pooper. Everyone is rich and getting richer, so there is nothing to worry about. All these people can't be mistaken, can they?

They can. All good things must come to an end. The government has decided to quit creating money for awhile because its inflation has led to double-digit price rises. No more new money is being created, so no new money is available for the Destitutionville real estate market. Prices stop rising.

Of course you don't mind the temporary cooling off period. You have a big fat profit, and you are content to wait for the government to start printing money again.

However, the last group of people who bought property have no profits. They bought when prices were already high, and they haven't earned one thin dime. They decide that Destitutionville isn't such a good place to invest after all, so they start selling their property.

Now the panic to get into Destitutionville turns into a panic to get out. You notice prices are starting to fall but you are not worried because you can afford to take a slight loss. But prices keep falling and you eventually join the panic. Unfortunately, by that time you cannot sell your property; no one is dumb enough to buy when prices are falling. Also, the number of new apartments is so large that half of them are unrented, and rents are falling (supply and demand again).

No matter how low you set your selling price, no one will buy, so you finally realize that your property is worthless. You've not only lost your $45,000 profit, but you've also lost your original $5,000.

Now you are stuck with your worthless property, and you must continue paying taxes on it hoping that someday the government will reinflate enough for you to get your $5,000 back.

After a few years you realize that the Destitutionville real estate market will probably never recover. You sell your apartments for $200 to a local farmer who tears them down and uses the land to plant corn.

You have learned the hard way that get-rich-quick is usually followed by get-poor-quick. But don't feel alone. Every time politicians inflate, millions of people get suckered into fast-money schemes.

Let's look at this a little closer. Before the inflation starts, some prices are already rising (while some are falling). Every healthy economy has some rising prices because some goods or services are always in shorter supply than others. A rising price is a signal to business people that more of a particular product is needed, and profits are available to anyone who satisfies that need.

When the inflation hits, lots of people are looking for good places to invest their extra dollars; they naturally flock to the investments that are already rising in price — causing these prices to rise further. More people invest, and the prices rise even more. Prices continue to skyrocket until the supply of new money dries up.

In other words if, for instance, apples are in short supply when an inflation starts, you can expect the price of apples to go far, far above anything reasonable. Those apples will draw money like a magnet draws iron filings.

If inflation is running at five or ten percent, the price of apples might rise at the rate of fifty or a hundred percent, maybe more. That's because the apples are noticeable; their rising price makes them stand out. They appear to be a better investment than other things, and they become fashionable, an investment fad.

Of course, the apples might indeed be a good investment if — and this is a big if — your timing is correct. You must buy at the right time and sell at the right time. And it is possible. Some people earn handsome incomes by doing nothing but buying and selling at the right times. They know how to profit from the boom-and-bust cycle.

Unfortunately, many other people earn tickets to the poor house by trying to do that. Your timing must be extraordinary.

One of history's best examples of the boom-and-bust cycle is the Great Stock Market Crash of 1929. All during the late 1920s people had been pouring money into the stock market. Then the government stopped creating money, and the supply of new dollars dried up. The same people who stampeded into the stock market started stampeding out. In only a few days, thousands of rich people became poor.

A similar incident, one of the strangest, happened in Holland about 350 years ago. It was called tulipmania.

Thousands of the Dutch were looking for a get-rich-quick scheme, and they discovered the idea of investing in tulips. There were so many people buying tulips and expecting to resell them for a profit that the price of tulips went almost straight up.

In 1637, the average annual wage in Holland was around 300 guilders. One variety of tulip went for 6,000 guilders per tulip. In terms of average U.S. wages in 2004, this would be about $670,000 per tulip.

Of course, after a few years the tulipmania stopped, and prices came back down to reasonable levels. People who sold out before the insanity ended made a fortune. But most of the investors lost a great deal.

If you don't want to be like the victims of 1929 or of tulipmania, either stay away from get-rich-quick fads or be very careful. Learn everything there is to know about your investments. Become an expert about them and about economic history—because it repeats—and remember that big rewards usually carry big risks. Above all, never trust anyone else to watch your investments for you; no one cares about you as much as you do, so no one is going to be as watchful as you are.

And, you'll need the courage of a riverboat gambler because that's the business you'll be in: gambling.

Speaking of business and investments, you might consider starting your own business. Many types of businesses require very little cash to get into. This might be the best investment you can make. Be your own boss. If you do it wisely, your risks will be lower and your rewards far greater than with any other kind of investment.

Most businesses and investment portfolios can be made almost immune to the effect of the inflation-recession "boom-and-bust" business cycle.   In fact, when the right strategy is used, they can generate enormous profits from the cycle.  The system is called Business Cycle Management or BCM.  (After I finish this set of letters on economics I'll write you in depth about BCM.[12])

Consider starting a business.  The economic turmoil is growing, and a business is probably the best way for a young person to get ahead.  Good Luck!

Uncle Eric

---

[12] For an indepth explanation of Business Cycle Management, read Richard J. Maybury's book THE CLIPPER SHIP STRATEGY, an Uncle Eric book, published by Bluestocking Press, phone 800-959-8586, web site: www.BluestockingPress.com

# 10

# The Boom and Bust Cycle

Dear Chris,

With gold and silver eliminated from our money, no one is quite sure what is money and what isn't. Many definitions are used. One, M2, defines money as currency, checking accounts, travelers checks, savings accounts, money market mutual funds, and certain transactions between banks.

If we subtract price increases from M2, we get the "real" M2 money supply.

Each time the government slows the creation of real M2, a recession hits.

The 1982 recession was the worst since the Great Depression. To end it, officials inflated the money supply heavily between 1983 and 1986. Some of this new money went into stocks[13] causing the stock market to rise. This caught the

---

[13] "Stock" refers to shares of ownership of a company. For instance, if you own one share of stock in a company that has issued ten shares, you own one-tenth of the company. If you own two shares, you own one-fifth of the company. Stock markets are the places where shares of stock are bought and sold. Terminology can sometimes be confusing. In the U.S., investors usually refer to "stocks." In Britain they refer to "shares." Both mean the same thing—a portion of the ownership of a company.

attention of millions of investors. They climbed on the bandwagon. Stocks became fashionable, a fad.

Much of the new money was channeled into the stock market causing an enormous boom; the market shot from 777 in 1982 to 2722[14] in 1987.

When inflation of M2 was slowed in 1987, the supply of new money to the stock market dried up. We got one of the worst stock market crashes in history and eventually a recession.

Uncle Eric

---

[14] Dow Jones Industrial Average. Begun in 1884 and published daily beginning in 1896 when the average price of an industrial stock stood at $35. In 1987 it was $2,722 per industrial stock.

# 11

# How Much is a Trillion?

Dear Chris,

You said you've been studying the federal debt (the so-called national debt) and are having trouble understanding its size, which, at the time I write this letter, is $12.110 trillion,[15] that's

$$\$12,110,000,000,000$$

Frankly, I believe the only people able to understand the federal debt now are astronomers. I'm serious. The federal debt has become so huge that it can be grasped only by persons who are comfortable discussing the number of light years spanned by our galaxy. This is why so few politicians worry about the debt. They've made it so big that it is no longer *real* to them; it's just meaningless numbers. But I'll try to help you get a handle on it.

---

[15] To find the current federal debt, conduct an internet search for U.S. National Debt Clock or U.S. Debt Clock. (As I write this today, current URLs are: DefeatTheDebt.com, www.brillig.com/debt_clock, and www.usdebtclock.org. You will discover that the federal debt per citizen on $12.110 trillion is $39,310 and per taxpayer is $111,290.

Do you consider one million dollars to be a lot of money? Imagine what you could buy with it. Make a list.

Now visualize $1 million in $100 bills laid end-to-end. You would need 20 minutes to walk the length of this line of cash; it's about one mile.

Walk a line of $100 bills the length of the federal debt and it would take you 390 years. This line of $100 bills would circle the earth 411 times.

If Columbus, when he stepped ashore in America, had immediately begun borrowing money at the rate of $20,000 per minute, by the year 2010, he would still not have borrowed the equivalent of today's federal debt. Here's another way to try to grasp the federal debt. A thousand one dollar bills tightly stacked is about four inches high. A million one dollar bills is 333 feet high. A trillion is 63,000 miles high.

Something happened in the early 1980s. Apparently officials made a deliberate decision to borrow without limit, to wallpaper the world with their bonds. (A bond is an IOU.)

How will they repay these bonds?

How will they pay the interest on them?

What do you think?

Uncle Eric

*Cherish public credit. One method of preserving it is to use it as sparingly as possible.*

**—George Washington
First President of the U.S.**

# Beyond the Basics

## The Roaring '90s

During the 1990s the Federal Reserve injected about 2.4 trillion new dollars[16] into the economy. Much of this new money went into the stock market. This created the greatest stock market boom in history, even greater than that of the 1920s.

The vast profits from the stock boom yielded vast increases in taxes for governments, enabling them to spend without borrowing. So, by the end of the decade the U.S. government's debt stopped growing.

Money poured into the pockets of stock investors triggering a huge spending spree. Sales of goods and services were strong, and employers had to hire more workers to produce them. Unemployment fell.

By 2000, federal officials had begun to slow their inflation of the money supply. Stocks crashed, and the 2001 recession began.

The inflation of the money supply that ended the 2001 recession then led to the great crash of 2008.

---

[16] According to the M3 Money Supply. (See page 134 for an explanation of M3 Money Supply.)

# Federal Debt Chart

During the 1980s, the federal government's uncontrolled tax-and-spend policy became an uncontrolled tax-and-borrow-and-spend policy.

Officials took 194 years to accumulate their first trillion dollars of debt and only five years to accumulate their second trillion. In 1990 they scored their third trillion, and in 1992 their fourth. As I write this today, they are working on their thirteenth.[17]

About 40% of individual income taxes now go solely for interest payments on the federal debt.[18] Obviously this cannot go on forever. What do you think the government will do?

Remember, governments have no real **wealth** of their own, they have only what they have taken from others.

---

[17] See www.usdebtclock.org

[18] "Taking the National Debt Seriously," by Lawrence Kadish, Wall Street Journal, 12 October 09, p. A17.

# Federal Debt
## (The so-called national debt)

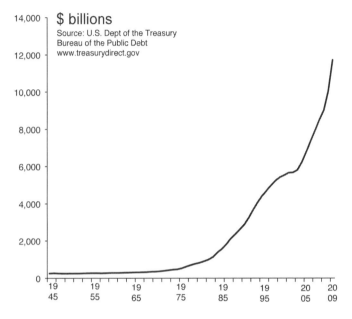

*During the 1990s, to pay for its runaway spending, the federal government was borrowing money at the rate of a million dollars every two minutes. After that, the rate doubled. Then during 2008 and 2009, the rate hit three million dollars every minute.*

**DEFICITS.** The shortfall between the government's income (taxes) and its spending. The shortfall is covered either through borrowing or printing money.

**FEDERAL DEBT** is the total of all federal deficits.

**NATIONAL DEBT** is federal debt.

# 12

# What's So Bad About the Federal Debt?

Dear Chris,

"You certainly are pessimistic," said the talk show host who interviewed me recently.

Yes, I'm pessimistic about America's future for the next ten years or so, but this doesn't mean individuals cannot be exceptions. They can learn enough history and economics to see what's coming and prepare for it, even profit.

I'm most pessimistic about the fortunes of the young. Good jobs have been scarce for them.

Why? A job is primarily the *tools* necessary to produce what others want to buy. A man with a $100,000 hydraulic backhoe can dig far more ditches than one with a $20 shovel. He can earn much higher wages and do more for his family.

Where does money for tools come from? Savings. Someone saves the $100,000 and puts it in stocks, bonds, or bank CDs (certificates of deposit) where it is available for businesses to use. Businesses acquire this money, buy the equipment, and hire workers.

If the $100,000 isn't saved, or if it is borrowed and spent by the government, it is not available to businesses. The backhoe isn't purchased and the worker is stuck with the $20 shovel and low wages.

In the U.S. today the average worker uses about $228,000 worth of tools.[19] But the government's spending has been so much greater than its income that it has been borrowing more than three million dollars per minute. This soaks up money that should be going to businesses for tools to create jobs.

Divide three million dollars by $228,000. The government's deficit consumes 13.2 jobs every minute; it wipes out 6.9 million jobs per year.

And, this damage is from the *deficit* only. We cannot know how much savings is eaten directly by *taxes* but it's certainly a lot more. Savings have been declining. I'm sure the government is now so large and powerful it is consuming more than ten million jobs annually.

Former U.S. Treasury Secretary William Simon called this "the great American seed corn banquet." When a farmer harvests a crop he saves a portion as seed to plant for next year's crop. If this seed is eaten...

This is not to say there will be fewer jobs. It is to say there will be fewer high-paying jobs. You will always be able to get a job digging ditches with a shovel for a dollar an hour. But high-paying jobs come from high savings, and government is consuming the savings.

Affluent members of the over-the-hill generation won't be hurt too badly, but the young are absolutely dependent on a steady supply of good jobs and our huge, voracious government is eating these jobs.

Uncle Eric

---

[19] Net stock of private fixed assets by industry, Statistical Abstract of the U.S., divided by number of Americans employed.

# An Interesting Exercise

Until the 1970s, most families were able to improve their standard of living with only one adult working outside the home. In the 1970s, '80s, and '90s, mothers and wives got paying jobs usually on the assumption they were helping support their families.

Try this. Add up the total taxes your household pays: state and federal income tax, sales tax, property tax, and any others you can find (remember that many taxes are "hidden taxes" that aren't easy to identify). Compare the total taxes paid with the total wages earned.

Chances are you will find that one spouse is supporting the household, and the other is supporting the government.

# One Reason Governments Spend So Much

Industries generally develop in three stages. First is scientific feasibility, second is engineering feasibility, and third is economic feasibility.

Using the airline industry as an example, the question in the 1800s was: "Is long-distance air travel possible?"

In the 1800s, balloons were already in use, but they were not practical. The problem to solve was the heavier-than-air machine.

In 1903, the Wright Brothers proved scientific feasibility. They risked their time, money, and lives to show that a heavier-than-air machine could fly.

In 1927, Charles Lindbergh proved engineering feasibility. He risked time, money, and his life to show that long-distance air travel was possible.

This gave investors enough confidence to risk their money in the aircraft industry. In 1935, the Douglas Company came out with the DC-3, which was the beginning of economic feasibility.

The modern airline industry resulted from all this risk-taking. Today, a middle-class American can go anywhere in the world much faster and in much greater comfort than a Roman emperor could. Travelers fly because the benefits are greater than the costs. This is economic feasibility.

This three-step model explains why governments are terrible at economic development. The "experts" who comprise the government gamble with other people's money, so they tend to confuse scientific and engineering feasibility with economic feasibility.

    Once science and engineering prove something can be done, those who comprise the government will do it—even if the costs are greater than the benefits.

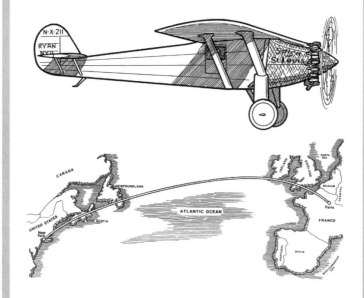

*In 1927 Charles Lindbergh proved engineering feasibility. He risked time, money, and his life to show that long-distance air travel was possible.*

# 13

# Summary

Dear Chris,

I'm almost finished with this set of letters, so I want to summarize what I've told you about inflations and recessions.

1. Inflation is an increase in the amount of money. When the amount of money goes up, the value goes down. When the value goes down, people need more of it. Rising prices are not inflation; they are a result of inflation. The wage/price spiral is a result, not a cause, of inflation.

2. At bottom, inflation is an ethics problem. It is a result of The Lie that is popular with voters. The Lie is, I will give you what you want, and you will never need to pay for it; I will force someone else to pay for it.

3. Inflation causes business people to make mistakes. When the inflation stops, the business people see their mistakes and start making corrections. They must lay off workers, and unemployment goes up.

4.     If the inflation starts up again, the corrections stop and the workers go back to work. A recession has happened.

5.     If the inflation does not start up again, the corrections are completed. Unemployment stays up for a longer time because the workers cannot go back to their old jobs; they must find new ones. That's a depression.

6.     Inflation causes recessions and depressions. The only way to have no recessions or depressions is to never inflate. Once inflation has started, there is no known way to avoid the results.

Chris, I hope one of the things my letters have taught you is that history is not just a collection of names, dates, wars, and revolutions. History is a logical sequence of events. You don't need to be a professional historian to understand it, and once you do understand it, you will be better able to cope with the events of today.

In my opinion, the quickest and easiest way to understand history is to study the history of money, especially gold and silver. This is because money is a mirror of civilization. Throughout history, whenever we find good, reliable noninflated money, we almost always find a strong, healthy civilization. Whenever we find unreliable, inflated money, we almost always find a civilization in decay.

The quality of the money reflects the quality of the ethics.

The most dramatic example I know of is Europe's Dark Ages. During the Dark Ages, all of Europe was in a terrible, poverty stricken condition; we might call it the biggest and longest (about 500 A.D. to 1000 A.D.) depression in the

# What Happened in 2008?

After **9-11**[20], the government created dollars to help pay for the war. Between 9-11 and August 2008, the money supply rose anywhere from 21% to 65%, depending on how it is measured.[21]

Newly created money must go somewhere. Much of it flowed into real estate, causing the largest real estate bubble in world history.

During bubbles, when money is flowing freely, investors often develop a casino mentality. They take much larger risks than they otherwise would. Their financial behavior becomes irrational. Remember the tulipmania of the 1600s. It was caused by expansion of the money supply.[22]

After 9-11, real estate became the new tulips. Millions of people bought homes and other properties they could not afford. In 2004, government officials became worried and began raising interest rates to dampen the frenzy. Higher interest rates make it difficult to buy a property. But the gambling mania was so intense the bubble did not burst until 2008, causing the most severe recession since the 1930s Great Depression. Officials were shocked by the depth of the crash, and began inflating the money supply wildly.

---

[20] On Sept. 11, 2001, in an attack against the U.S., over 3,000 civilians were murdered. The World Trade Center, a portion of the Pentagon, and four civilian airliners were destroyed.

[21] St. Louis Federal Reserve web site. Monetary base, 30%; M1, 21%; MZM, 65%; M2, 46%.

[22] "The Truth About Tulipmania," by Doug French, Ludwig von Mises Institute website, 26 May 07.

history of mankind. A major reason the Dark Ages lasted so long is that the feudal governments were brutal and crooked, and there was no money that was reliable enough to be widely accepted. (The money of the Roman Empire had decayed along with the Empire.) The lack of reliable money made production and trade very difficult, so people were unable to lift themselves above the poverty level.

It wasn't until good, reliable money like the thaler began to circulate that Europe came out of its Dark Ages.

Today, if you travel around the world you will find that the countries that have the best money, like New Zealand and Switzerland, also have the healthiest economies. Those countries are good places to live. The countries that have the worst money (see the C.I.A. World Factbook web site) also have the weakest economies. I would not like to live there.

This brings up an interesting question. Does good money create a healthy civilization or does a healthy civilization create good money? Which comes first, the chicken or the egg?

I believe TANSTAAFL comes first. I have noticed that whenever and wherever the money begins to turn rotten, someone (either voters, or politicians, or both) has been ignoring the fact that you can't get something for nothing.

Chris, when that happens, these people stop trying to produce what they need. They start looking for tricks and gimmicks, which usually means stealing or inflation in order to get what they need.

On the other hand, whenever and wherever people respect the fact that we cannot have more unless we produce more, the money stays solid and the civilization stays healthy. That's because the specialization of labor that makes civilization possible can only happen when good reliable money exists.

In other words, don't believe the popular saying about money being the root of all evil.[23] On the contrary, money is the foundation of our whole world. If we respect that foundation and make it solid, there will be almost no limits to what we can accomplish.

When I say almost no limits, I am not exaggerating. Have you ever heard of the "German Miracle?" That "miracle" is living proof that we can accomplish almost anything if we make wise economic decisions.

At the end of World War II, Germany was in ruins; much of it had been bombed back into the Dark Ages. A great deal of the housing had been destroyed, millions of workers had been killed, and the lines of transportation and communication had been demolished. Entire cities had been leveled and whole industries had disappeared. The money was hyper-inflated so badly that it was worthless.

Wage/price controls, which had been started by the Nazis and rigidly enforced by the Gestapo during the war and by the military governors after the war, had created a black market. But even the black market was unable to supply the people with enough food, clothing, or other necessities.

People were reverting to barter, and they were leaving the cities to go out into the countryside where they could forage for food. In some places the poverty and famine were so bad that the people had returned to the Stone Age.

As if all that trouble were not bad enough, Germany was overrun by immigrants, 8.5 million of them, who were fleeing from the countries that had been captured by the Russian government.

---

[23]"Money is the root of all evil" is a common misquote of "The love of money is the root of all evil."

I once met a woman who was in Germany during that time, and she told me about some of the things that happened to her. The robberies, murders, poverty, and famine were terrible, as bad as the war itself. Most of her family died, and she was very lucky to have survived.

No one knew how to solve Germany's problems; no one, that is, except a small group of economists led by a man named Ludwig Erhard. Erhard was able to persuade the people who were governing Germany that the wage/price and other controls must be lifted. He also convinced them that taxes must be lowered and inflation must be stopped.

Most controls were lifted, taxes were lowered dramatically, and a new, hard (noninflated) currency, the Deutschmark, was introduced. Almost overnight things got better. People who had been stealing and killing began working, and people who had abandoned the cities came back. Everyone knew that their hard work would be rewarded with **hard money** and the things hard money would buy. An eyewitness said:

> Shops filled up with goods from one day to the next; the factories began to work. On the eve of currency reform the Germans were aimlessly wandering about their towns in search of a few additional items of food. A day later they thought of nothing but producing them. One day apathy was mirrored in their faces while on the next a whole nation looked hopefully into the future.

Germany not only came out of the Dark Ages but by 1960 the country had fully recovered. By 1970, it was one of the world's most prosperous nations. In the short span of 25 years, the German people went from barbaric poverty and chaos to a very high standard of living, a low rate of inflation, and a low unemployment rate. They owed it almost entirely to Ludwig Erhard and his fellow economists.

Unfortunately the "German Miracle" was confined to Germany. Other countries, like Britain, did not follow Erhard's advice. Although they ended the war in much better shape than Germany and received as much help from other countries as Germany, they have often been worse off than Germany with more inflation and unemployment. It's really a shame.

So what about our future? Next letter.

Uncle Eric

# The Unknown Shakeout[24]

In World War II, military production shot from about 2% of total U.S. output to an astounding 38%.

As soon as Tokyo surrendered, most of this military capacity became unneeded. It was the equivalent of malinvestment, and had to be corrected.

The federal government did not meddle in the correction. The "shakeout" was widely seen as part of the war effort, the final price Americans would need to pay for victory.

The managers of Sears believed the shakeout would be mild, and began to expand. Their rival, Montgomery Ward, believed the U.S. would fall back into the Great Depression, and became very cautious.

The Sears team turned out to be right.

Montgomery Ward never recovered from its mistake. The company eventually went broke, in 2000.

Unencumbered by government meddling, the postwar correction was swift. In only three years, the military's 38% of total production dropped to 4% (today it's about 5%). Yet, despite this colossal wave of retooling, rebuilding, retraining and relocation of workers, unemployment rose to only 5.9% at its worst. (The 2001 recession drove it to 6.3% and the 2008 recession went over 10%).

---

[24]From Richard Maybury's U.S. & World Early Warning Report Newsletter for Investors. August 2009.

The corrections required today need to be very broad. The money supply has been so heavily inflated for so many decades that there probably isn't anything in the U.S. that is in the right place, doing what it should, at the correct prices.

But it's hard to believe the corrections need to be as deep as those of the 1940s.

In 1945, almost all the country's heavy industry was geared for making war goods. Production of civilian automobiles was illegal. The 3.5 million square foot Willow Run plant in Michigan—Charles Lindbergh called it the Grand Canyon of the mechanized world—employed 42,000 workers and turned out a four-engine B-24 bomber every hour.

With the stroke of a pen in Tokyo Bay on the morning of September 2, 1945, fully 89% of this Himalaya of "Big Iron" became unneeded and had to be shaken out. But—my key point—the disruption was so mild that few people today even know it happened.

However, unlike recessions now, the post-WWII recession was seen not as a problem but a solution, and it was allowed to proceed unhindered.

Today, recessions are seen as problems. As in the Great Depression, the government tries to stop them, by throwing mountains of money at them. And so, like the Great Depression, recessions drag on and on, and complete corrections do not happen.

# 14

# Where Do We Go From Here?

Dear Chris,

As I said before, no other inflation in history has been as widespread (almost worldwide) as the present one. We don't know exactly what to expect, but we can make some guesses.

Unfortunately, so few people understand what is happening that things may not change for a long time. It is possible that we'll keep going down this same inflationary path until we have a runaway inflation. It could take many years, maybe decades, but maybe not. If people become so fearful that velocity shoots up, a runaway inflation can develop in just weeks.

However, if enough people learn what is happening, we do have a good chance to get out of this without too much damage.

I believe modern communication and transportation are swift enough to make the necessary corrections very fast and easy. If people order their governments to stop inflating, we might get through the depression very quickly, within a year.

The biggest hazard is impatience. If people get in a hurry, they may demand that the politicians interfere with the businesspersons' corrections. That's what happened in the 1930s, and it made the Great Depression a very long one. It caused the wrong corrections; then the corrections had to be corrected. It was a mess. There were more unemployed people in 1940 than in 1931. That's how beneficial Franklin Roosevelt's "New Deal" was.

For instance, people asked Mr. Roosevelt to make employers stop firing workers. The President did. But some business people didn't have enough money to keep paying all their workers. Instead of only a few workers losing their jobs, the businesses went broke and many workers lost their jobs.

People also asked the government to prevent foreign businesses from selling goods in the U.S. (and people in other countries were asking their governments for the same favor). The government did what the people asked—so foreign companies could not sell their products. They had to fire workers, and the depression spread around the world, getting worse and worse.

Fortunately this is not the 1930s. We understand better what is happening now. If enough people can be taught what causes the "boom-and-bust" business cycle, then maybe we can stop it, at least for a while.

We can learn a lesson from Ancient Greece. For many decades, voters in Athens elected only the politicians who would take an oath against debasing the money. The oath was taken every twelve months. It stopped the inflation and depressions, and Athens became a very rich city. Life was pleasant for many years.

In the Byzantine Empire, people were so afraid of inflation and depression that anyone who clipped coins had his hand cut off. It was cruel, but it worked. For a time there was no inflation or depression. In fact, the Byzantine coin, the bezant, stayed valuable for a thousand years. It was probably the best money in history; people were glad to have it because they knew its value would not fall.

I want to share a lesson I've learned.

You'll notice a lot of people like to blame their enemies for the inflation and recessions. Republicans blame Democrats, labor blames management, one ethnic group blames another, poor people blame rich people, and so forth. As prices and unemployment go up, hatred spreads. A person starts hating people he's never even met.

Be careful you don't fall into this trap. It has destroyed a lot of people and a lot of countries. For example: In some areas of Europe, the money lending, banking, and other financial work is done mostly by Jewish people. This is because Christians in these areas believe the Bible tells them not to do that kind of work. Therefore, in some towns, the only people who understand money are Jewish.

During World War I, when one of the German runaway inflations started, only a few Germans knew enough about money to know what would happen and prepare for it. They were mostly Jewish. Compared to everyone else they were wealthy.

When Hitler came to power, he made speeches about Jews being the only rich people in Germany. He said the Jews caused the Germans' troubles in order to get rich from them. That's how Hitler was able to start persecuting the Jews.

Due to lack of education, these kinds of things happen over and over again because people think economics is too hard to understand.

Instead of learning what is happening and what to do about it, they just get mad. Then they start looking for revenge. They go on "witch hunts."

We haven't seen the last of inflations, recessions, or depressions, so be sure you aren't part of any "witch hunts." Learn more about economics. I suggest you write The Foundation for Economic Education, Irvington-On-Hudson, New York, 10533. Tell them who you are, how you heard about them, and that you'd like to learn more about economics.

Remember TANSTAAFL. (There ain't no such thing as a free lunch.) And spread the word.

Uncle Eric

# Beyond the Basics

# 15

## Natural Law
## and Economic Prosperity

Dear Chris,

In my last letter I encouraged you to learn more about economics.

However, in this final letter I want to encourage you to learn about law.

Economics and law are both very important to your economic prosperity and individual liberty. Let me explain.

In my work I have put years of research into examining different societies to determine which had the most liberty as well as the greatest economic prosperity.

What I am about to tell you is vitally important to your financial future and should influence whatever investment decisions you make. If you remember nothing else from this last letter, remember the following: *A country's economic prosperity, or lack of it, is directly related to its legal system.*

Understanding the legal system that leads to liberty and prosperity is so important that I promise to send you an entire set of letters regarding this subject very soon.[25] Until that time, I want to briefly introduce the subject to you now, so you can begin to think about it.

At bottom, Chris, there are two types of law. One is Natural Law,[26] represented by the old English common law. The premise of Natural Law is that there is a Higher Law than any government's law, and a judge's job is to discover and apply this Higher Law.

Under Natural Law,[27] an individual's rights to his life, freedom, and property are granted not by the government but by, in the words of the American Declaration of Independence, the "Creator." No human authority can reduce these rights.

The Natural Law system grows out of the two fundamental laws taught by all religions: 1) do all you have agreed to do (this is the basis of contract law), and 2) do not encroach on other persons or their property (this is the basis of tort law and some criminal law).

Any law logically consistent with these two laws is valid. Any "law" not logically consistent with them is not.

Experience shows that where these laws are widely obeyed by everyone, including the government, the result is liberty, free markets, and rapid economic growth. Investment and job opportunities abound.

---

[25] Uncle Eric is referring to Richard J. Maybury's book WHATEVER HAPPENED TO JUSTICE?, an Uncle Eric book, published by Bluestocking Press, web site: www.BluestockingPress.com, phone 800-959-8586.

[26] Natural Law, as it is used in Richard J. Maybury's Uncle Eric books, has no connection with the Natural Law Party. Natural Law is an ancient legal term.

[27] In this context, Higher Law and Natural Law are taken to mean the same thing.

The other basic type of legal system is generally referred to as civil law or Roman law.[28] Its premise is that there is no law higher than the government's law and an individual's rights are granted by the government. A judge's job is to apply the government's law no matter what this law requires, even if the government's law violates the two fundamental laws.

Civil law or Roman law can lead to liberty and free markets, or it can lead to slavery. Lawmakers are free to do whatever they believe necessary—no exceptions, no limits.

They can allow free press, free speech, and free markets one week, then change their minds and throw millions into concentration camps the next week. Whatever appears necessary.

Throughout recorded history, civil law has been the dominant system around the world. However, for about seven centuries, from the Magna Carta in 1215 to World War I and the Great Depression, much of the world was moving in the direction of Natural Law.

After 1776, America became the leader of this movement to Natural Law. Countries that adopted a Natural Law viewpoint came to be known as the "free world," of which America was the acknowledged leader. These countries also became the most prosperous, with the most job opportunities, the largest middle classes, and the most investment opportunities.

During these seven centuries, even nations that had Roman systems inherited directly from Rome itself—for instance, Italy and France—began to shift in the direction of

---

[28] For a complete explanation of Roman law, read Richard J. Maybury's book ANCIENT ROME: HOW IT AFFECTS YOU TODAY, an Uncle Eric book, published by Bluestocking Press, phone 800-959-8586, web site: www.BluestockingPress.com.

Natural Law. The more closely they adhered to the two fundamental laws, the more their economies grew, yielding unprecedented abundance.

Chris, I should point out that the law of the Roman Republic was an early form of common law. It was based on the premise that there is a Higher Law than any government's law, and the court should try to discover and apply this law.

But the Roman Republic was replaced by the Roman Empire, and the law of the empire is what was reborn in the 20$^{th}$ century—whatever appears necessary. The law we call Roman law or civil law is actually a throwback to the primitive type of law Rome had before the Republic.

Unfortunately, in the mid-1800s, **socialism**[29] began to spread and, by about 1960, it had become the dominant political and economic philosophy in nearly every nation.

The movement to Natural Law died away. Today, in America, few know anything about Natural Law or why it leads to economic advancement.

Socialism does not work, and by 1990 its failure had become apparent. Wherever it had been tried the result was economic decline. The textbook case was the Union of Soviet Socialist Republics.

However, and this is my key point, Chris, socialist economics has been rejected. After the fall of the USSR, socialist economics was rejected in almost every nation. Freer markets became a popular goal. But the never-ending desire for a free lunch did not vanish and, by the end of the 1990s, socialist ideas were making a comeback.

---

[29] Socialism. An economic and political system under which virtually everything and everyone is owned and controlled by government agencies. Marxism.

In 2003, the U.S. government was led by Republicans, who tend to not like socialism. But they enacted Medicare Part D, one of the largest socialist programs in history.

In 2008 and 2009, the recession was so frightening that practically the whole country demanded huge new socialist measures.

Worse, not only is socialist economics making a comeback, but socialist law, meaning Roman law or civil law, remains entrenched and *continues* to grow everywhere— including America. Nearly everyone has been taught to believe that lawmakers should do whatever appears necessary, without regard to ethical principles. The two fundamental laws have been almost completely forgotten everywhere.

So, the move to free markets is not the historic paradigm shift[30] its fans like to think it is. It is only an experiment based on expediency, not ethics.

When lawmakers find that free market policies cut deeply into their power, they are not happy about it. We have already seen the results in Venezuela's return to statism[31] in 1992 and in China at the Tianamen Square massacre in 1989. Lawmakers re-asserted their power. In 1997, Belarus became the first nation of the former USSR to officially and openly revert to dictatorship.

---

[30] Paradigm shift means a change in the model of how the world works. To read more about models, read Richard J. Maybury's book UNCLE ERIC TALKS ABOUT PERSONAL, CAREER, AND FINANCIAL SECURITY, an Uncle Eric book, published by Bluestocking Press, phone: 800-959-8586, web site: www.BluestockingPress.com

[31] Statism: The opposite of the original American philosophy. Says political power is a good thing. Government is our friend, our protector, the solution to our problems, and there is no law higher than the government's law.

Chris, dozens of nations are conducting free market experiments, but in every case these experiments can be easily reversed. *Those that run the highest risk of reversal are the ones with legal systems based on Roman law (civil law).*

So you see, Chris, economics is just part of the formula that leads to liberty and economic prosperity. The other part is law.

Roman law enables governments to inflate their currencies and tax without limit.

Chris, someday you will begin to invest your money, but before you invest in a foreign country be sure to check the country's legal system. It is the single most important determinant of the country's economic growth and the safety and profitability of your investments.

Mainstream financial organizations pay little or no attention to legal systems, so I will give you a quick explanation, then a list of the legal systems of some 200 countries.

This is not to say you should avoid investing in these nations, Chris. You might make a lot of money riding the wave of free market experimentation. *But the type of legal system tells you a lot about the amount of risk you are taking.* The less Natural Law, the more swiftly and suddenly the free market experiment can be terminated.

Conversely, the more rigorously a nation's legal system applies the two fundamental laws to everyone—including the government—the less risk you run when you invest there.

This is not just my opinion. In THE ECONOMIST magazine dated April 19, 1997, you can read the article "The Law of the Market" that confirms it. Says the article, "The results of this analysis are stark. First, the economists find, common-law countries are far more protective of shareholders than civil-law countries."

Chris, when you invest in any nation, including America, scrutinize that nation closely and don't get into anything you cannot get out of fast (in a day or two). If that nation has no heritage of Natural Law, watch even more closely and be even quicker to bail out at the first sign of trouble.

A civil law system that has not been influenced by Natural Law is a time bomb virtually certain to wreck the economy and whatever investment you have there.

Under civil law, or Roman law, the government is exempt from the two fundamental laws. It might obey them, but only as a courtesy, not an obligation.

Under civil law, the government is also a third party to all contracts. It can change any contract at any time without the consent of the other parties. It does not even need to notify the other parties, although it may do so as a courtesy.

Chris, following this letter is a list of nations and their types of legal systems. *This list is unique—you will not find it anywhere else.*

Where I say "English common law," this should always be read as "*based* on English common law," or Natural Law (or Higher Law). No nation today practices a pure form of common law or Natural Law, but some are better than others. Examples of the best are New Zealand, America, Switzerland, Britain, Australia, and Canada. This is not to say these are the best places to make a quick profit. They simply offer the least risk of a sudden political change that could wipe you out.

Perhaps the top example of a legal system based on Natural Law was Hong Kong's system prior to the Chinese takeover on July 1, 1997.

Whenever possible, along with the type of legal system for each country, I have included the country's Index of Economic Freedom as reported in the 2009 INDEX OF ECONOMIC FREEDOM by Terry Miller, Kim R. Holmes, published by The Heritage Foundation and the *Wall Street Journal*.

The INDEX OF ECONOMIC FREEDOM should be on every investor's bookshelf and every investor should be thoroughly familiar with it. It gives you a detailed easy-to-understand report on the extent of economic freedom in each country. You can find it on the Heritage Foundation web site.

The best possible score is 100; the worst is 1.

At the time I write this, the top position in the INDEX OF ECONOMIC FREEDOM is Hong Kong with a score of 90.0. The worst position is North Korea with a score of 2.0. Updates of these scores are available at the following web site: http://www.heritage.org/Index/Ranking.aspx (or search the Heritage Foundation web site).

| **Best Scores** | **Worst Scores** |
| --- | --- |
| Hong Kong, 90.0 | Sao Tome and Principe, 43.8 |
| Singapore, 87.1 | Libya, 43.5 |
| Australia, 82.6 | Comoros, 43.3 |
| Ireland, 82.2 | Dem. Rep. of Congo, 42.8 |
| New Zealand, 82.0 | Venezuela, 39.9 |
| United States, 80.7 | Eritrea, 38.5 |
| Canada, 80.5 | Burma, 37.7 |
| Denmark, 79.6 | Cuba, 27.9 |
| Switzerland, 79.4 | Zimbabwe, 22.7 |
| United Kingdom, 79.0 | North Korea, 2.0 |

Checking the legal system and Index of Economic Freedom gives you a quick, but highly revealing, look at the investment potential of any given country. Those with heavy Natural Law influence and economic freedom indexes of 75.0 to 80.0 are likely to have the least risk.

In general, they are also safer places to travel as a tourist or businessperson. Before you visit any country, check its index to see how much risk you are taking.

Always remember—*a country's economic prosperity, or lack of it, is directly related to its legal system.*

As I said earlier, I will provide you with another set of letters[32] to explain in greater detail the system of Natural Law and its importance to economic prosperity and liberty.

In the meantime, Chris, remember that the very best protection for future investments is a population that is dedicated to the two fundamental laws and tolerates no violation of them. Spread the word to everyone you care about.

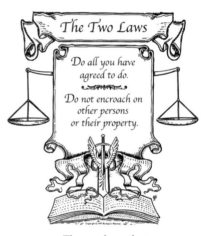

*The two laws that make civilization possible.*
**Spread the Word!**

And, if you find a country in which no violation of the two laws is tolerated, please let me know. I'd like to move there.

Uncle Eric

---

[32] Uncle Eric is referring to WHATEVER HAPPENED TO JUSTICE? by Richard J. Maybury, an Uncle Eric book, published by Bluestocking Press, phone: 800-959-8586, web site: www.BluestockingPress.com

# Beyond the Basics

## Nations and Legal Systems

Colonial law means the law of the European power that dominated the country when the country was a colony. This law was not usually identical to the European law. For instance, it normally contained special privileges for the Europeans and provisions to keep the natives "in their place." When the Europeans were overthrown, the special privileges were erased or sometimes reversed to keep the Europeans "in their place."

Islamic law is law derived from the Koran (the Islamic holy book). Strict Islamic law contains the two fundamental laws but adds much more, for example, in some locations, prohibitions on charging interest on loans and requiring women to remain fully covered head to toe.

At the time I write this, nations without index numbers are not rated in the INDEX OF ECONOMIC FREEDOM.[33] Sometimes this is because they are very small. Other times it is because they are so chaotic they have no systems to rate.

---

[33] INDEX OF ECONOMIC FREEDOM by Terry Miller, Kim R. Holmes, published by The Heritage Foundation and the *Wall Street Journal*. At the time I write this, updates of these scores are available at the following web site: http://www.heritage.org/Index/Ranking.aspx

**Afghanistan.** Embroiled in war since 1979, Afghanistan has little real law. The meager amount it does have is a mixture of sharia (Islamic common law) overlaid by a thin layer of western law imposed by Washington after 9-11. Chaos. Stay away. (not ranked)

**Albania.** Civil law. Very little Natural Law influence. **63.7**

**Algeria.** Mixture of French colonial civil law and Islamic law. Not influenced by Natural Law. **56.6**

**Andorra.** Civil law, French and Spanish.

**Angola.** Civil law, mostly Portuguese. Not influenced by Natural Law. **47.0**

**Anguilla.** Based on English common law.

**Antigua and Barbuda.** Based on English common law.

**Argentina.** Originally a constitution and common law system similar to that of America, but now heavily Roman. Some Natural Law influence. **52.3**

**Armenia.** Civil law. Not influenced by Natural Law. **69.9**

**Aruba.** Dutch civil law mixed with some English common law.

**Ashmore and Cartier Islands.** Based on English common law, Australian.

**Australia.** Based on English common law. **82.6**

**Austria.** Civil law, with constitution heavily influenced by Natural Law. **71.2**

**Azerbaijan.** Civil law. Not influenced by Natural Law. **58.0**

**Bahamas.** Based on English common law. **70.3**

**Bahrain.** Mixture of Islamic law and English common law. **74.8** (but look out for Persian Gulf wars and revolutions).

**Bangladesh.** Based on English common law; Islamic influence. **47.5**

**Barbados.** Based on English common law. **71.5**

**Belarus.** Civil law. Not influenced by Natural Law. **45.0**

**Belgium.** Civil law, heavily influenced by Natural Law. **72.1**

**Belize.** Based on English common law. **63.0**

**Benin.** Based on French colonial civil law. **55.4**

**Bermuda.** Based on English common law.

**Bhutan.** A former British and Indian puppet regime. Based on English common law and Indian law. **57.7**

**Bolivia.** Civil law, Spanish and Napoleonic. Slight Natural Law influence. **53.6**

**Bosnia.** Civil law. No real Natural Law influence. **53.1**

**Botswana.** Civil law mixed with Dutch and local native law. **69.7**

**Brazil.** Civil law, with slight Natural Law influence. **56.7**

**British Virgin Islands.** Based on English common law.

**Brunei.** Islamic law.

**Bulgaria.** Civil law. Almost no Natural Law influence. **64.6**

**Burkina Faso.** Based on French colonial civil law. **59.5**

**Burma.** Chaotic, heavily socialistic. Not influenced by Natural Law. **37.7**

**Burundi.** Mixture of German and Belgian civil law, with some local native law. **48.8**

**Cambodia.** Chaotic, not identifiable. Not influenced by Natural Law. **56.6**

**Cameroon.** Based on French colonial civil law, with slight Natural Law influence. **53.0**

**Canada.** Based on English common law, except in Quebec, which is French civil law. **80.5**

**Cayman Islands.** Based on English colonial common law.

**Central African Republic.** Based on French colonial civil law. **48.3**

**Chad.** Based on French colonial civil law and some local native law. **47.5**

**Chile.** Based on Spanish, French, and Austrian civil law. Some Natural Law influence. **78.3**

**China.** Chaotic. Very socialist. Some local customary law. Not influenced by Natural Law. Much like Russia—each town is a separate de facto country with its own legal system. **53.2**

**Columbia.** Based on Spanish colonial civil law and some U.S. law. **62.3**

**Comoros.** Mixture of French colonial civil law and Islamic law. **43.3**

**Congo, Republic of.** Mixture of French colonial civil law and local native law. **45.4**

**Congo, Democratic Republic of.** Mixture of Belgian colonial civil law and local native customary law. Chaotic. Stay away. **42.8**

**Costa Rica.** Based on Spanish colonial civil law. Slight Natural Law influence. **66.4**

**Croatia.** Civil law with heavy socialist influence. No sign of Natural Law. **55.1**

**Cuba.** Mostly socialist civil law, with a smattering of U.S. law. All traces of Natural Law have been erased. **27.9**

**Cyprus.** Mixture of common law and civil law. **70.8**

**Czech Republic.** Based on Austro-Hungarian civil law, with recent Natural Law influence. Reason for hope. **69.4**

**Denmark.** Civil law, with strong Natural Law influence. **79.6**

**Djibouti.** Based on French colonial civil law, Islamic law, and some local native law. **51.3**

**Dominica.** Based on English colonial common law. **62.6**

**Dominican Republic.** Based on French colonial civil law. **59.2**

**Ecuador.** Civil law. Slight Natural Law influence. **52.5**

**Egypt.** Mix of English colonial common law, civil law, and Islamic law. **58.0**

**El Salvador.** Civil law, with traces of Natural Law. **69.8**

**Equatorial Guinea.** Based on Spanish colonial civil law and some native law. **51.3**

**Eritrea.** Very unsettled. Will probably be some mixture of Italian, British, and Islamic. **38.5**

**Estonia.** Civil law. Some Natural Law influence. **76.4**

**Ethiopia.** Very unstable. Civil law, with heavy socialist influence. **53.0**

**Fiji.** Based on English colonial common law, but unsettled due to military coups. **61.0**

**Finland.** Civil law, with heavy Natural Law influence. **74.5**

**France.** Civil law, with heavy Natural Law influence. **63.3**

**French Guiana.** Based on French colonial civil law.

**French Polynesia.** Based on French colonial civil law.

**Gabon.** Based on French colonial civil law and native customary law. **55.0**

**Gambia.** Combination of English colonial common law, Islamic law, and native customary law. **55.8**

**Georgia.** Civil law. Wars. Chaos. No Natural Law influence. **69.8**

**Germany.** Civil law, with heavy Natural Law influence. **70.5**

**Ghana.** Based on English colonial common law and native customary law, with heavy socialist influence. **58.1**

**Greece.** Roman law, with some Natural Law influence. **60.8**

**Grenada.** Based on English colonial common law.

**Guatemala.** Civil law. **59.4**

**Guinea.** Based on French colonial civil law and native customary law. **51.0**

**Guyana.** Mixture of English colonial common law and Dutch civil law, with heavy socialist influence. **48.4**

**Haiti.** Based on civil law. Highly corrupt. **50.5**

**Honduras.** Mostly civil law, with slight Natural Law influence. **58.7**

**Hong Kong.** Until the Chinese takeover on July 1, 1997, it was perhaps the world's best application of Natural Law. After July 1, 1997, see China. **90.0**

**Hungary.** Civil law, with some Natural Law influence. **66.8**

**Iceland.** Danish civil law, with heavy Natural Law influence. **75.9**

**India.** Based on English colonial common law, with heavy civil law (socialistic) influence. **54.4**

**Indonesia.** Based on Dutch civil law, mixed with native customary law. **53.4**

**Iran.** Islamic law with socialist controls. Corrupt. Chaotic. **44.6**

**Iraq.** Combination of Islamic law and civil law. Thin layer of western law imposed by Washington. Everything very unsettled. A high risk place. (not ranked)

**Ireland.** Based on English common law and native customary law. **82.2**

**Israel.** Mixture of English colonial common law, Jewish law, and some Islamic and Christian law. **67.6**

**Italy.** Roman law, with heavy Natural Law influence. **61.4**

**Ivory Coast.** Based on French colonial civil law and some local native law. (not ranked)

**Jamaica.** Based on English colonial common law. **65.2**

**Japan.** Civil law, with American Natural Law influence imposed by General Douglas MacArthur after World War II. Will this imposed Natural Law hold? **72.8**

**Jordan.** Combination of French colonial civil law and Islamic law. **65.4**

**Kazakhstan.** Civil law. Not influenced by Natural Law. **60.1**

**Kenya.** Mixture of English colonial common law, Islamic law, and native law. **58.7**

**Kirgizstan.** Civil law.

**Korea, North.** Combination of German civil law, Japanese civil law, and socialist civil law. Not influenced by Natural Law. **2.0**

**Korea, South.** Combination of European civil law, American Natural Law, and Chinese civil law. **68.1**

**Kuwait.** Combination of civil law and Islamic law. **65.6**

**Laos.** Civil law. Not influenced by Natural Law. **50.4**

**Latvia.** Civil law, with Natural Law influence. **66.6**

**Lebanon.** Mixture of French civil law and Ottoman civil law. **58.1**

**Lesotho.** Mixture of English colonial common law and Dutch civil law. **49.7**

**Liberia.** Mixture of American Natural Law and native customary law. **48.1**

**Libya.** Mixture of Italian colonial civil law and Islamic law. **43.5**

**Liechtenstein.** Civil law, with heavy Natural Law influence. (not ranked)

**Lithuania.** Civil law, with some Natural Law influence. **70.0**

**Luxembourg.** Civil law, with heavy Natural Law influence. **75.2**

**Macau.** Portuguese civil law. **72.0**

**Macedonia.** Civil law. **61.2**

**Madagascar.** Mixture of French colonial civil law and native customary law. **62.2**

**Malawi.** Based on English colonial common law and native customary law. **53.7**

**Malaysia.** Based on English colonial common law. **64.6**

**Maldives.** Based on English colonial common law and Islamic law. **51.3**

**Mali.** Based on French colonial civil law and native customary law. **55.6**

**Malta.** Mixture of English common law and civil law. **66.1**

**Mauritania.** Mixture of Islamic law and civil law. **53.9**

**Mauritius.** Mixture of English colonial common law and French civil law. **74.3**

**Mexico.** Civil Law, with some American Natural Law influence. Heavily socialistic. **65.8**

**Moldova.** Civil law. Not influenced by Natural Law. **54.9**

**Monaco.** Based on French civil law, with heavy Natural Law influence. (not ranked)

**Mongolia.** Mixture of Russian, Chinese, and Turkish civil law. Not influenced by Natural Law. **62.8**

**Montenegro.** Civil law, with very slight Natural Law influence. **58.2**

**Morocco.** Mixture of French civil law, Spanish civil law, and Islamic law. **57.7**

**Mozambique.** Based on Portuguese civil law. Heavily socialistic. **55.7**

**Namibia.** Based on Dutch civil law. **62.4**

**Nepal.** Mixture of English colonial common law and Hindu law. **53.2**

**Netherlands.** Civil law, with heavy Natural Law influence. **77.0**

**New Zealand.** Based on English common law. One of the best. **82.0**

**Nicaragua.** Civil law. Chaotic. **59.8**

**Niger.** Based on French colonial civil law and native customary law. **53.8**

**Nigeria.** Based on English colonial common law, Islamic law, and native law. **55.1**

**Norway.** Civil law, with heavy Natural Law influence. **70.2**

**Oman.** Based on English colonial common law and Islamic law. **67.0**

**Pakistan.** Based on English colonial common law, with Islamic influence. Much local variation. Chaotic. **57.0**

**Panama.** Civil law, with some American Natural Law influence. **64.7**

**Papua New Guinea.** Based on English colonial common law. **54.8**

**Paraguay.** Civil law, with a trace of Natural Law. **61.0**

**Peru.** Civil law, with a trace of Natural Law. **64.6**

**Philippines.** Mixture of Spanish civil law and American Natural Law. **56.8**

**Poland.** Civil law, with holdover socialist law and some Natural Law influence. **60.3**

**Portugal.** Civil law, with some Natural Law influence. **64.9**

**Qatar.** Mixture of Islamic and civil law. Whatever the amir (chief) thinks necessary. **65.8**

**Romania.** Civil law. Very little Natural Law influence. **63.2**

**Russia.** Nominally, civil law, but central control has faded and each town is a de facto, separate country, with its own civil law that changes whenever local rulers decide to change it. Very little Natural Law influence. Chaos. **50.8**

**Rwanda.** Mixture of German and Belgian colonial civil law and local native customary law. **54.2**

**Saint Kitts and Nevis.** Based on English colonial common law.

**Saint Lucia.** Based on English colonial common law. **68.8**

**Saint Vincent and the Grenadines.** Based on English colonial common law. **64.3**

**San Marino.** Civil law with heavy Natural Law influence.

**Sao Tome and Principe.** Mixture of Portuguese civil law and local native customary law. **43.8**

**Saudi Arabia.** One of the strictest Islamic law countries, with some influence from civil law. **64.3**

**Senegal.** Based on French colonial civil law. **56.3**

**Serbia.** Civil law, with very slight Natural Law influence. **56.6**

**Seychelles.** Mixture of English colonial common law, French colonial civil law, and local native customary law. **47.8**

**Sierra Leone.** Mixture of English colonial common law and local native customary law. **47.8**

**Singapore.** Based on English colonial common law. A great success story. **87.1**

**Slovak Republic.** Civil law, with signs of Natural Law influence. **69.4**

**Slovenia.** Civil law, with some Natural Law influence. **62.9**

**Somalia.** Whatever the local warlord decides. Chaos, stay away. (not ranked)

**South Africa.** Mixture of Dutch colonial civil law and English colonial common law. **63.8**

**Spain.** Civil law with Natural Law influence. **70.1**

**Sri Lanka.** Mix of English colonial common law, Dutch colonial civil law, Islamic law, and local native customary law. **56.0**

**Sudan.** Islamic law, with remnants of English colonial common law. (not ranked)

**Swaziland.** Mixture of South African Dutch civil law and local native customary law. **59.1**

**Sweden.** Civil law, with heavy Natural Law influence. **70.5**

**Switzerland.** Civil law, with heavy Natural Law influence. One of the best. **79.4**

**Syria.** Mixture of civil law and Islamic law. **51.3**

**Taiwan.** Civil law, with some Natural Law influence. **69.5**

**Tanzania.** Based on English colonial common law. **58.3**

**Thailand.** Mixture of civil law and some common law. **63.0**

**Togo.** French colonial civil law. **48.7**

**Tonga.** Based on English colonial common law. **54.1**

**Trinidad and Tobago.** Based on English colonial common law. **68.0**

**Tunisia.** Mixture of French colonial civil law and Islamic law. **58.0**

**Turkey.** Mixture of European civil law systems. Much popular pressure for more Islamic influence. **61.6**

**Turkmenistan.** Civil law. No Natural Law influence. **44.2**

**Uganda.** In transition to a mix of local native customary law and, hopefully, English common law. **63.5**

**Ukraine.** Civil law. Very little Natural Law influence. **48.8**

**United Arab Emirates.** Mixture of Islamic law and civil law. **64.7**

**United Kingdom.** English common law, heavily influenced by civil law. **79.0**

**United States.** Based on English common law. The original Natural Law premise has been almost totally erased and replaced by civil law. But the Bill of Rights still provides a lot of protection against the government. The Bill of Rights is, however, about the only part of the legal system that still does, and each time Congress meets, more of it is chipped away. The war that began 9-11 has accelerated the undermining of the Bill of Rights. **80.7**

**Uruguay.** Based on Spanish colonial civil law. **69.1**

**Uzbekistan.** Civil law. No Natural Law influence. **50.5**

**Venezuela.** Civil law. **39.9**

**Vietnam.** Mixture of French colonial civil law and socialist law. **51.0**

**Yemen.** Mixture of Islamic law, English colonial common law, Turkish law, and local native customary law. **56.9**

**Zambia.** Based on English colonial common law and local native customary law. **56.6**

**Zimbabwe.** Mixture of Dutch colonial civil law and English colonial common law. **22.7**

# Appendix

Excerpt from THE LONG WINTER ................................. 123
Sutter's Fort Trade Store Sign ................................. 124
Comparison of Law Chart ........................................ 125
Distilled Wisdom .................................................... 126
**The Truth About Inflation** ................................... **131**
The Oil Myth ........................................................... 133
**Measures of Money Supply** ................................... **134**
Supply of Dollars Chart ........................................... 135
**Real Wages** ......................................................... **136**
Real Wages Chart .................................................... 137
**How to Invest in Gold and Silver** ......................... **138**
Resources ............................................................... 139
Movies and Documentaries ..................................... 141
**Internet Addresses** ............................................. **142**
**Financial Newsletters** .......................................... **144**
Bibliography and Recommended Reading ............. 145
Glossary ................................................................. 150

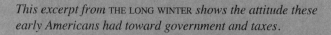

*This excerpt from* THE LONG WINTER *shows the attitude these early Americans had toward government and taxes.*

*Excerpted with permission of*
*Roger Lea MacBride from*

# The Long Winter
by Laura Ingalls Wilder

Mr. Edwards admired the well-built, pleasant house and heartily enjoyed the good dinner. But he said he was going West with the train when it pulled out. Pa could not persuade him to stay longer.

"I'm aiming to go far West in the spring," he said. "This here country, it's too settled-up for me. The politicians are a-swarming in already, and ma'am if'n there's any worst pest than grasshoppers it surely is politicians. Why, they'll tax the lining out'n a man's pockets to keep up these here county-seat towns! I don't see nary use for a county, nohow. We all got along happy and content without 'em.

"Feller come along and taxed me last summer. Told me I got to put in every last least thing I had. So I put in Tom and Jerry, my horses, at fifty dollars apiece, and my own yoke, Buck and Bright, I put in at fifty, and my cow at thirty-five.

"'Is that all you got?' he says. Well, I told him I'd put in five children I reckoned was worth a dollar apiece.

"'Is that all?' he says. 'How about your wife?' he says.

"'By Mighty! I says to him. 'She says I don't own her and I don't aim to pay no taxes on her.' I says. And I didn't."

"Why, Mr. Edwards, it is news to us that you have a family." said Ma. "Mr. Ingalls said nothing of it."

"I didn't know it myself," Pa explained. "Anyway, Edwards, you don't have to pay taxes on your wife and children."

"He wanted a big tax list," said Mr. Edwards. "Politicians, they take a pleasure a-prying into a man's affairs and I aimed to please 'em. It makes no matter. I don't aim to pay taxes. I sold the relinquishment on my claim and in the spring when the collector comes around I'll be gone from there. Got no children and no wife, nohow."

# Sign posted in Trade Store
# at Sutter's Fort State Historic Park
### Sacramento, California

Courtesy of the Sutter's Fort Living History Program. This document
represents composite information and is not original to the Fort.

---

# Notice

Discounting of Currency

1.       All Paper Currency drawn upon State Banks and State
Offices of Comptrollers will be discounted 45% Per
Centum on Transactions. There will be no Exceptions.

2A.      Mexican and British Bank Drafts will be Discounted
27% Per Centum on Transaction.

2B.      All Bank Drafts on Pacific Coast Merchants, Banks,
Lending Houses, and Ships Pursuers will be
discounted 33% Per Centum on all Transactions.

3.       All Bank Drafts and Letters of Credit or Exchange,
on European Merchants, Banks, Lending Houses or
Governmental Agencies doing Business on this
Coast and redeemable in Silver or Gold will be
discounted at 15% or Exchanged at a 20% Discount.

4.       All Coinage will be Exchanged or Accepted at Face
Value minus 5% on Volume of Business Transactions.
Banking of Funds on Sandwich Island Accounts
Payable — 5% of Volume.

Drafts and Warrants upon this establishment will be
1.       Accepted at Face Value for Trades — or — at 10%
Discount for Exchange of Coin or Drafts of Letters of
Credit.

By Order of
John A. Sutter
Proprietor

January 14, 1846  George N. Loker
                         Chief Clerk

---

*The value of the money was reduced according to the risk of accepting
it. Store owners preferred money that was likely to retain its value.*

## Comparison of Law Chart
*Reprinted from* WHATEVER HAPPENED TO JUSTICE? *by Richard J. Maybury*
Natural Law or Common Law was the origin of the original American philosophy, but America has now switched to political law, which is a Roman concept.

| Scientific Law *(Natural Law or Common Law)* | Political Law *(Legislation)* |
|---|---|
| **Requirements** | |
| Based on fact, logic, and the two fundamental laws: 1) do all you have agreed to do, and 2) do not encroach on other persons or their property. | Whatever the powerholders decide. |
| "All men are created equal"—no special exemptions or privileges.[34] | Whatever the powerholders decide. |
| Cautious and hesitant in the use of force. | Whatever the powerholders decide. |
| **Characteristics** | |
| Predictable, knowable. | Whimsical. |
| Evolutionary change. Few reversals. | Frequent revolutionary changes. Many reversals. |
| Discovered by judges, one case at a time. | Made up by politicians in response to political pressure and "influence." |
| Highly developed, advanced. | Primitive. |
| **Results** | |
| Tends to neutralize political power. | Gives powerseekers more power. |
| Creates liberty and security. | Destroys liberty and security. |
| Makes effective economic calculation possible—spurs creation of wealth and abundance. | Uses force to redistribute wealth. Destroys incentive to produce wealth. |
| Stable economic environment. | Boom-and-bust cycles. |
| Enables civilization to advance. | Destroys civilizations. |

[34] Applies to all mentally competent adults, whether acting as individuals or in groups. The problem of children and mentally incompetent adults remains unsolved under both systems.

# Distilled Wisdom

## Political Power and Government

Government is not reason, it is not eloquence; it is force! Like fire, it is a dangerous servant and a fearful master.
**—George Washington, 1732-1799**
First President of the United States

The people never give up their liberties but under some delusion.
**—Edmund Burke, 1729-1797**
British statesman

Rightful liberty is unobstructed action according to our will within limits drawn around us by the equal rights of others. I do not add 'within the limits of the law,' because law is often but the tyrant's will, and always so when it violates the rights of the individual.
**—Thomas Jefferson, 1743-1826**
Author of the Declaration of Independence

I am more and more convinced that man is a dangerous creature; and that power, whether vested in many or a few, is ever grasping, and, like the grave, cries 'Give, give.'     **—Abigail Adams, 1744-1818**
Wife of President John Adams

America is great because America is good. When America ceases to be good, America will cease to be great.
**—Alexis de Tocqueville, 1805-1859**
Sociologist

It is strangely absurd to suppose that a million human beings collected together are not under the same moral laws which bind each of them separately.     **—Thomas Jefferson**

Sometimes it is said that man cannot be trusted with the government of himself. Can he, then, be trusted with the government of others?

**—Thomas Jefferson**

Every time government attempts to handle our affairs, it costs more and the results are worse than if we had handled them ourselves.

**—Benjamin Constant, 1833-1891**
Brazilian statesman

There are severe limits to the good that the government can do for the economy, but there are almost no limits to the harm it can do.

**—Milton Friedman, 1912-2006**
Nobel laureate

Never blame a legislative body for not doing something. When they do nothing, that don't hurt nobody. When they do something they can be dangerous.

**—Will Rogers, 1879-1935**
Humorist and columnist

He has erected a multitude of new offices, and sent hither swarms of officers to harass our people, and eat out their substance.

**—Declaration of Independence, 1776**

In politics we are most ruthless when we are trying to be altruistic.

**—Anonymous**

The history of liberty is a history of limitation of government power, not the increase of it.

**—Woodrow Wilson, 1856-1924**
28th President of the United States

The pleasure of governing must certainly be exquisite, if we may judge from the vast numbers who are eager to be concerned with it.

**—Voltaire, 1694-1778**
French writer

# Inflation & Paper Money

The loss which America has sustained since the peace, from the pestilent effects of paper money on the necessary confidence between man and man, on the necessary confidence in the public councils, on the industry and morals of the people, and on the character of republican government, constitutes an enormous debt against the states chargeable with this unadvised measure.                                    **—James Madison, 1751-1836**
Architect of U.S. Constitution

That paper money has some advantages, is admitted. But that its abuses also are inevitable, and, by breaking up the measure of value, makes a lottery of all private property, cannot be denied. Shall we ever be able to put a constitutional veto on it?                **—Thomas Jefferson**

You have to choose (as a voter) between trusting the natural stability of gold and the honesty and intelligence of members of the government. And with due respect for these gentlemen, I advise you, as long as the capitalist system lasts, to vote for gold.
**—George Bernard Shaw, 1856-1950**
Playwright & Novelist

The best way to destroy the capitalist system is to debase the currency.
**—Nikolai Lenin, 1870-1924**
Socialist founder of the Soviet Union

A wagon-load of money will scarcely purchase a wagon-load of provisions.                                              **—George Washington**

There is no subtler, or surer means of overturning the existing basis of society than to debase the currency. The process engages all the hidden forces of economic law on the side of destruction, and does it in a manner which only one man in a million is able to diagnose.
**—John Maynard Keynes, 1883-1946**
Economist

# Taxes & Government Spending

Now what liberty can there be where property is taken without consent?
**—Samuel Adams, 1722-1803**
American Revolutionary and Leader of the Boston Tea Party

The public money of this country is the toil and labor of the people, who are under many uncommon difficulties and distresses at this time, so that all reasonable frugality ought to be observed.
**—John Adams, 1735-1826**
American Revolutionary and Second President of the United States

If we run into such [government] debts, as that we must be taxed in our meat and in our drink, in our necessaries and our comforts, in our labors and our amusements, for our callings and our creeds, as the people of England are, our people, like them, must come to labor sixteen hours in the twenty-four, give the earnings of fifteen of these to the government for their debts and daily expenses, and the sixteenth being insufficient to afford us bread, we must live, as they now do, on oatmeal and potatoes, have no time to think, no means of calling the mismanagers to account; but be glad to obtain subsistence by hiring ourselves to rivet their chains on the necks of our fellow-sufferers.          **—Thomas Jefferson**

We must then tell you that we will never submit to be hewers of wood or drawers of water for any ministry or nation in the world.
**—John Jay, 1745-1829**
American Revolutionary and co-author of THE FEDERALIST PAPERS

# Federal Debt

The question, whether one generation of men has a right to bind another, seems never to have been started. ... [I believe] no generation can contract debts greater than may be paid during the course of its own existence. ... The conclusion then, is, that neither the representatives of a nation, nor the whole nation itself assembled, can validly engage debts beyond what they may pay in their own time.          **—Thomas Jefferson**

If the debt should once more be swelled to a formidable size, its entire discharge will be despaired of, and we shall be committed to the English career of debt, corruption and rottenness, closing with revolution.
**—Thomas Jefferson**

Cherish public credit. One method of preserving it is to use it as sparingly as possible.                                   **—George Washington**

Avoiding likewise the accumulation of debt, not only by shunning occasions of expense, but by vigorous exertions in time of peace to discharge debts which unavoidable wars may have occasioned, not ungenerously throwing upon posterity the burden which we ourselves ought to bear.
**—George Washington**

## Commerce and Wealth

In transactions of trade it is not to be supposed that, as in gaming, what one party gains the other must necessarily lose. The gain to each may be equal. If A has more corn than he can consume, but wants cattle; and B has more cattle, but wants corn; exchange is gain to each; thereby the common stock of comforts in life is increased.     **—Benjamin Franklin, 1706-1790**
Signer of the Declaration of Independence

The statesman who should attempt to direct private people in what manner they ought to employ their capitals would not only load himself with a most unnecessary attention, but assume an authority which could safely be trusted, not only to no single person, but to no council or senate whatever, and which would nowhere be so dangerous as in the hands of a man who had folly and presumption enough to fancy himself fit to exercise it.
**—Adam Smith, 1723-1790**
Economist

Property is the fruit of labor; property is desirable; is a positive good in the world. That some should be rich shows that others may become rich, and hence is just encouragement to industry and enterprise. Let not him who is houseless pull down the house of another, but let him work diligently to build one for himself, thus by example assuring that his own shall be safe from violence when built.     **—Abraham Lincoln, 1809-1865**
16th President of the United States

# Beyond the Basics

## The Truth About Inflation

Fuzzy language causes fuzzy thinking. We cannot understand events in the economy or investment markets if we fail to use words with clear meanings.

During the 1800s, it was common knowledge that the word inflation meant an increase in the number of dollars (or marks, francs, pounds, etc.).

People also knew that money responds to the law of supply and demand just as everything else does. As the number of dollars increases, the value of each individual dollar falls. Prices rise to make up for this fall.

Rising prices are not inflation. They are a result of inflation.

When crooks expand the money supply, this is called counterfeiting. When governments do it, it is called "monetary policy," but it is the same thing, inflation. In both cases it causes devalued money and rising prices.

Few governments want us to understand what they are doing. Most have redefined inflation to mean rising prices. This draws attention away from the money supply.

In the U.S., the most popular measure of so-called inflation is the government's Consumer Price Index, or CPI. The CPI tries to measure the average prices of items consumers buy.

For instance, if you left a supermarket with a shopping bag containing a $5.00 magazine, a $2.00 loaf of bread, and a $1.00 pair of shoelaces, the average price of the items you bought was $2.67.

If next week the price of the shoelaces goes to $1.50 and the loaf of bread to $2.50, then the average price of the items in your shopping bag would rise to $3.00.

To compute the CPI, the government tracks the prices of hundreds of items consumers buy and reports on this monthly.

During the 1990s, the CPI rose little, not more than three percent per year. Government officials were able to gleefully print money, causing an economic boom, while boasting that inflation was under control.

Those of us who earn our livings trying to peer through the fog of government propaganda were doubtful. We were pointing out that consumers buy more than food, clothing, and the other items in the CPI. They also buy stocks (shares of ownership in corporations).

Officials omit stocks from the CPI, apparently on the assumption that stock prices are not prices.

If they are not prices, what are they?

Some economists have long argued that if stocks were included in the CPI, the CPI would be much more complete and would better reflect the true change in prices from the government's inflation.

There's more. Consumers buy another item that is highly expensive but is not in the CPI. In fact, it is by far the most costly thing they buy, even more costly than food or housing.

It is government. Consumers spend more of their incomes on government, in the form of taxes, both hidden and unhidden, than on anything else.

# The Oil Myth

A widespread myth claims inflation can be caused by rising oil prices. Supposedly, oil is such an important source of energy that it is involved in the production of almost everything, and when its price goes up, all other prices do, too.

This is really a half-truth. For goods comprised mostly of oil—plastics, for instance—it's quite true. A sharp rise in oil prices will cause a sharp rise in plastic prices.

But for most goods the price of oil is only a very small percentage of the total price. For example, the electricity used by all the carpenters and other workmen who build a $200,000 house is less than $20.00. If an increase in oil prices were to cause a massive tripling of electricity prices, this would add only $40 to the price of the $200,000 house. The price of the house would increase only 0.02%, and this is typically the case throughout most of the economy.

If neither the money supply nor velocity are increasing, the overall price level cannot increase.

If oil prices rise, and people are spending more money on oil-related items, they will have less to spend on other things. The prices of these other things will fall. The overall price level will remain unchanged.

The only way for rising oil prices to lead to an increase in the overall price level is for someone to print money to pay for the oil, or for velocity to rise.

# Beyond the Basics

## Measures of Money Supply

How can the total amount of money be measured? No one knows, but economists and bankers work on the problem constantly.

One problem is that when gold and silver vanished from the currency so did agreement about what money is. Most include paper currency, coins, and checking accounts, but beyond this few are sure. How about savings accounts? Credit/debit cards? Travelers checks? Money market funds?

Another problem is that different definitions seem to work best at different times. Until the 1980s, the M1 measure was most widely used. Then M2 became popular. In the 1990s, many began using a new measure called MZM. In the new decade M3[35] seems to be gaining much favor.

Here are the definitions of the seven most commonly used measures, listed from narrowest to most broad:

Currency. The narrowest measure, coins and paper dollars held by the public (not in the government's vaults).

Monetary Base. Currency + deposits in Federal Reserve Banks. Sometimes referred to as the raw material from which most U.S. money is made.

M1. Currency + checking accounts.

M2. M1 + savings accounts + money market mutual funds.

MZM. M2 minus small savings accounts (under $100,000), plus large institutional money funds.

M3. M2 + large certificates of deposit, institutional money market deposits, repurchase agreements, and Eurodollars (dollars outside the U.S.).

L. The broadest measure. Total liquid assts. M3 + other liquid assets including Treasury Bills, commercial paper, and savings bonds.

[35] The government has stopped disclosing M3 and L, but you can check the Shadow Government Statistics website by John Williams.

**Supply Of Dollars Circulating in the U.S.**

Using the M1 measure of money supply

billions

Source: Federal Reserve Bank of St. Louis - research.stlouisfed.org/fred2

The government's Federal Reserve banking system was created in 1913, and gold and silver were removed from the money in 1971. What did this do to the money supply?

# Beyond the Basics

## Real Wages

The "real" wage is the wage minus the effects of inflation. According to Bureau of Labor Statistics data, in the early 1970s, real wages in the U.S. began falling.

BLS data for "Total compensation," which includes not only wages but benefits such as paid vacations and insurance, show a rise, but this is misleading. On average, more than a third of the "benefits" are paid not to the employee but to the government, in the form of Social Security and other taxes which are distributed to persons all over the country. For these and other "benefits," the theory is that the employee will someday collect the full value. The theory may be true for older employees, but for those under age 40, or maybe even 50, it's a high risk bet surely few would be willing to make if they had an informed choice.

"Even for workers at the 90th percentile of earners—making about $80,000 per year—inflation has outpaced their pay increases … 'There are two economies out there,' Mr. Cook, the political analyst said. 'One has been just white hot, going great guns. Those are the people who have benefited from globalization, technology, greater productivity and higher corporate earnings. And then there's the working stiffs,' he added, 'who just don't feel they're getting ahead despite the fact that they're working very hard. And there are a lot more people in that group than in the other group.'"

—"Real Wages Fail to Match a Rise in Productivity"
NEW YORK TIMES BUSINESS website
August 28, 2006

# Real Wages

Average weekly earnings of production
workers, adjusted for inflation, using the
Consumer Price Index.

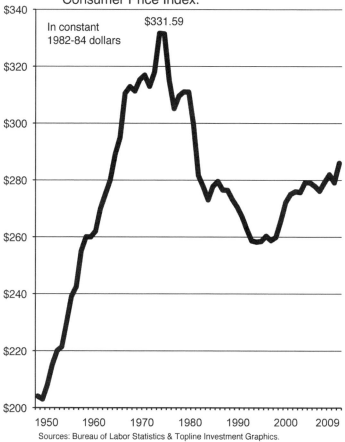

In constant
1982-84 dollars

$331.59

Sources: Bureau of Labor Statistics & Topline Investment Graphics.

# Beyond the Basics

## How to Invest in Gold and Silver

Gold and silver are financial insurance not only against severe inflation but also against all other kinds of turmoil. For thousands of years, through wars, revolutions, depressions, famines—even the fall of the Roman Empire and the Dark Ages—gold and silver have always retained at least some of their value. No other investment has done this. Some parcels of land will retain value, but it is impossible to know in advance which ones they will be.

In other words, gold and silver are financial bedrock. They survive when nothing else does.

A good way to own gold and silver is in the form of bullion coins like the American Eagle or the Canadian Maple Leaf.

As with everything else in life, before you buy, look around for the best deal. Call at least three gold and silver dealers to compare prices.

# Resources

*Listed below are sources of information about inflation, business cycles, economics, and related subjects for children and adults. Since URLs change frequently, it is suggested you conduct an internet search for their current URLs.*

Advocates for Self-Government, Inc., phone: 800-932-1776, www.theadvocates.org. A non-profit, non-partisan libertarian educational organization.

Audio Forum, phone: 800-243-1234, www.audioforum.com. Audio recordings on free market subjects (i.e. Milton Friedman, Murray Rothbard, and Ludwig von Mises).

Bluestocking Press, phone: 800-959-8586, web site: www.BluestockingPress.com. Publisher of the Uncle Eric series of books, written by Richard J. Maybury. According to William P. Snavely, Emeritus Professor of Economics at George Mason University, "The entire series should be a required, integral, component of the social studies curriculum in all public and private schools. This would bring a quantum leap upward in the quality of citizenship in this country in a single generation." The series includes: *1) Uncle Eric Talks About Personal, Career and Financial Security 2) Whatever Happened to Penny Candy? 3) Whatever Happened to Justice? 4) Are You Liberal? Conservative? or Confused? 5) Ancient Rome: How It Affects You Today 6) Evaluating Books: What Would Thomas Jefferson Think About This? 7) The Money Mystery 8) The Clipper Ship Strategy 9) The Thousand Year War in the Mideast: How It Affects You Today 10) World War I: The Rest of the Story and How It Affects You Today 11) World War II: The Rest of the Story and How It Affects You Today.* For ages 13 through adult. (Student study guides are available for most of the Uncle Eric books.)

Cato Institute, phone: 202-842-0200, http://www.cato.org  Cato's mission, per its web site, is to "increase the understanding of public policies on the principles of limited government, free markets, individual liberty, and peace."

Foundation for Economic Education, Inc., phone: 800-960-4FEE, www.fee.org. Fee is one of the oldest free-market organizations in the U.S. and offers a comprehensive educational program.

Knowledge Products, www.knowledgeproducts.net, phone: 800-729-2665, Interesting, well-produced stories about great economists and the importance of their ideas to our businesses, careers, and investments. Those on Austrian economics are especially important *(The Austrian Case for the Free Market Process* by Ludwig von Mises and Friedrich Hayek; *Early Austrian Economics* by Carl Menger, Eugen von Bohm-Bawerk, and other pioneers). High school through adult.

Laissez Faire Books, phone: 866-686-7210, www.lfb.org. Offers an extensive collection of books on liberty, free markets, economics, politics and history.

LibertyTree, phone: 800-927-8733, www.liberty-tree.org. A free market research and educational organization. Books and publications.

The Mint, www.themint.org. Information especially for young people about money and finance. From Northwestern Mutual.

Mises Institute, phone: 334-321-2100, http://mises.org. Austrian school of economics.

Talicor, Inc., phone: 800-433-GAME, web site: www.talicor.com. Source of *Made for Trade,* a board game in the free enterprise spirit. For ages 8 through adult.

# Movies and Documentaries with Good Economic History

*Since URLs change frequently, it is suggested you conduct an internet search for current URLs if required.*

**AMERICA'S CASTLES** series (DVD). Produced by the History Channel, shop.history.com. Highly recommended by Richard Maybury for its economic history.

**AUTOMOBILES** series (DVD). Produced by the History Channel, shop.history.com. Highly recommended by Richard Maybury for its economic history.

**CADILLAC DESERT, Part One.** Good economic and legal history. Originally available from PBS Home Video. Out of circulation. Look for this used.

**THE GREAT SHIPS: The Clippers** (DVD). Produced by the History Channel, shop.history.com. All videos in the series are recommended for their good economic history, but especially The Clippers. Excellent supplement to Richard Maybury's THE CLIPPER SHIP STRATEGY.

**GREED** (DVD) with John Stossell (3/11/99). An ABC News product, web site: http://abcnewsstorego.com. Dispells much of the myth about the greedy robber baron capitalist and explains how capitalism works through a system of voluntary exchange.

**TRAINS UNLIMITED,** copyright A&E Television Networks, aired on the History Channel. Out of circulation. Try finding this used. Highly recommended, especially the story of the Atchison, Topeka, and Santa Fe Railroad, the Harvey Hotels, and the employment of the Harvey girls. Good economic history showing how industries develop and how industries affect the development of towns and cities.

# Beyond the Basics

## Internet Addresses

*Internet addresses go out of date quickly but here are ones that might be useful at the time of this printing. Web sites change endlessly, and the mention of a site here does not necessarily mean Uncle Eric agrees with what you will find at the time you access the site. All can be located by conducting an internet search.*

**Freedom House Index** by Freedom House. Survey of political freedom in nearly all countries. www.freedomhouse.org

**Dictionaries.** Language dictionaries and technical dictionaries including economics. www.yourdictionary.com

**The Economist.** The world's best news magazine. Tends to be very good at economics, although it also promotes the usual British interventionist foreign policy. www.economist.com

**C.I.A. World Factbook.** Economic, political, and legal information about nearly all countries. https://www.cia.gov/library/publications/the-world-factbook/index.html

**Federal Reserve Bank of Saint Louis.** Economic data and links to other economic data sites. www.research.stlouisfed.org/fred2

**Index of Economic Freedom** by the Heritage Foundation. Survey of economic freedom in nearly all countries. www.heritage.org

## Investment sites

www.bloomberg.com

www.briefing.com

www.businessweek.com/finance

www.cbsmarketwatch.com

www.edgar-online.com

http://finance.yahoo.com

www.fool.com

www.investools.com

www.money.cnn.com

http://moneycentral.msn.com

www.morningstar.com

http://quicken.intuit.com

## Business and Economic Numeric Data

http://lib.mansfield.edu/subjects.cfm

## Buying gold

www.ngccoin.com

www.pcgs.com

See Richard Maybury's YouTube video on how-to-buy precious metals.

# Beyond the Basics

## Financial Newsletters

*These financial newsletter writers are familiar with the economic forces described in* WHATEVER HAPPENED TO PENNY CANDY? *and they take these forces into account when making recommendations. Since URLs change frequently, it is suggested you conduct an internet search for their current URLs.*

*The Aden Forecast,* Aden Research, PO Box 790260, St, Louis, MO 63179, phone: 305-395-6141

Jim Dines, *The Dines Letter,* PO Box 22, Belvedere, CA 94920, phone: 800-845-8259

*Dow Theory Letters,* PO Box 1759, LaJolla, CA 92038, phone: 858-454-0481

Ian McAvity, *Deliberations,* PO Box 182, Adelaide St. Station, Toronto, ON, Canada, M5C 2J1, phone: 416-964-1359

R.E. McMaster, *The Reaper,* PO Box 84900, Phoenix, AZ 85071, phone: 800-850-0583

Robert Prechter, *Elliot Wave International,* PO Box 1618, Gainesville, GA 30503, phone: 800-336-1618

Howard Ruff, *The Ruff Times,* PO Box 545, Ithaca, NY 14851

Mark Skousen, *Forecasts & Strategies,* One Massachusetts Avenue N.W., Washington, D.C. 20001, phone: 800-211-7661

Martin Weiss, Weiss Research, *Money and Markets* newsletter, 15430 Endeavor Dr., Jupiter, FL 33478, phone: 800-291-8545

# Bibliography
## and Recommended Reading

*If you would like to have a better understanding of the economic events which affect your life, this list is a good place to start. I suggest you* begin with CAPITALISM FOR KIDS; THE MONEY MYSTERY; THE CLIPPER SHIP STRATEGY; ECONOMICS IN ONE LESSON; THE INCREDIBLE BREAD MACHINE; I, PENCIL; and ECONOMICS: A FREE MARKET READER. *Thereafter, you should have no trouble selecting other works.*

*Many of these books and articles are more than a decade old. Notice how accurate the predictions have been. There isn't much happening today that was not foreseen. History repeats. Contact your librarian for locating out-of-print books.*

AMAZING ACHIEVEMENTS by Nigel Hawkes. Awe-inspiring feats that can create the faith that if humans can overcome these obstacles they can overcome any obstacles. A wonderful book. Published by Thunder Bay Press, San Diego, 1996. Out of print. For ages 13 and up.

AMERICA'S GREAT DEPRESSION by Murray N. Rothbard. A heavily documented textbook which details the 1920s inflation and 1930s depression. Distributed by the Ludwig von Mises Institute, Auburn, AL, www.mises.org/. For ages 17 and up.

"ARGENTINE DILEMMA" by H. J. Maidenberg. *The New York Times.* April 11, 1971. Describes inflationary events in Argentina. A preview of America's future? For ages 16 and up.

BETTER THAN A LEMONADE STAND by Daryl Bernstein. Written by the author when he was 15 years old, this book offers 51 businesses for young entrepreneurs to launch which require little or no start-up costs. Includes marketing tips and more. Published by Beyond Words Publishing, www.beyondword.com

COMMON SENSE BUSINESS FOR KIDS by Kathryn Daniels. A common sense first guide for young entrepreneurs about running a successful business. Published by Bluestocking Press, phone: 800-959-8586, web site: www.BluestockingPress.com. For ages 12 and up.

CAPITALISM FOR KIDS by Karl Hess. An outstanding introduction to entrepreneurship. Author Karl Hess stresses how a person can earn a profit in business while maintaining the highest possible standards of honesty and integrity. Includes a self-test to help the reader determine how enterprising he/she really is, as well as an excellent chapter on "Capitalism and Other Isms" which clearly defines capitalism, democratic socialism, socialism, and communism. Although written with young people in mind, many adults will benefit by reading this book, especially the section which was written specifically for parents and teachers. Published by Bluestocking Press, web site: www.BluestockingPress.com, phone: 800-959-8586. For ages 10 and up.

CONNECTIONS by James Burke. An excellent introduction to economic history. Notice that the parts of the world that brought forth the most advancement and improvement were those that contained the most liberty. Book published by Little, Brown & Co., Boston, 1978. DVDs distributed through PBS, www.shoppbs.org. For ages 13 and up.

ECONOMICS: A FREE MARKET READER edited by Jane A. Williams and Kathryn Daniels. A good understanding of free market economics may be gained by reading the articles in this book, which is an excellent supplement to A BLUESTOCKING GUIDE: ECONOMICS—the student study guide for Richard J. Maybury's book WHATEVER HAPPENED TO PENNY CANDY. Published by Bluestocking Press, phone: 800-959-8586, web site: www.BluestockingPress.com. For ages 12 and up.

ECONOMICS IN ONE LESSON by Henry Hazlitt. One of the best books on economics ever written. Very clearly and concisely exposes many cliches and fallacies. Published by Crown. For ages 14 and up.

ECONOMICS ON TRIAL by Mark Skousen. Analyzes ten economic textbooks and shows the fallacies on which they are based. Appropriate for high school level and above. Published by Business One Irwin, Homewood, IL. Out of print. For ages 16 and up.

ECONOMIST, THE. http://www.economist.com. Best single source of news and analysis of the world economy. Easier reading and more interesting than you might think. Weekly magazine. For ages 16 and up.

FIAT MONEY INFLATION IN FRANCE by Andrew Dickson White. The story of the great French inflation during the French Revolution. Published by Cornell University Library. For ages 14 and up.

FOR GOOD AND EVIL by Charles Adams. The impact of taxes on the development of civilization. How taxes have caused unemployment and poverty through the ages. Outstanding real history makes for fascinating reading. Published by Madison Books, London, 1993. For ages 14 and up.

FORTY CENTURIES OF WAGE AND PRICE CONTROLS by Robert Schuettinger and Eamonn Butler. Numerous examples of the failure of wage and price controls through the ages. Published by the Heritage Foundation, Washington, DC, 1979. For ages 14 and up.

GREAT INFLATION, GERMANY 1918-23, THE, by William Guttmann and Patricia Meehan. The story of the great German inflation after World War I. Published by Clifford Frost Limited, Wimbledon, England, 1975. ISBN 0-86033-035-4. For ages 14 and up.

HOW MUCH IS A MILLION and IF YOU MADE A MILLION by David M. Schwartz. Written and beautifully illustrated for young children, but probably revealing to many adults. Helps you grasp the size of a million, billion, and trillion. Makes the enormity of the government's debt more understandable—and frightening. Both are published by HarperCollins. For ages 7 and up.

HOW YOU CAN PROFIT FROM THE COMING DEVALUATION by Harry Browne. Don't let the sensationalistic ballyhoo on the cover scare you. The investment advice is outdated, but the first 100 pages contain an outstanding explanation of inflation, the business cycle, and the way the banks and Federal Reserve System work. Published by Avon Books, New York, NY. Out of print. For ages 14 and up.

"I, PENCIL" by Leonard Read. Reprinted from *The Freeman Magazine,* December 1958. A classic. An outstanding description of the free market's method of allocating resources. Put this at the top of your list. Available from the Foundation for Economic Education, Irvington-on-Hudson, NY. Also reprinted with permission in WHATEVER HAPPENED TO JUSTICE? and the BLUESTOCKING GUIDE: ECONOMICS, both published by Bluestocking Press. For ages 12 and up.

INCREDIBLE BREAD MACHINE, THE, by Susan Love Brown, et al. Written by and for college students. A clear, concise, entertaining look at economic issues. Published by Fox & Wilkes, San Francisco, CA 94103. Out of print. For ages 13 and up.

INDEX OF ECONOMIC FREEDOM. Published by The Heritage Foundation, Washington, D.C. Ages 12 and up.

INFLATION CRISIS AND HOW TO RESOLVE IT, THE, by Henry Hazlitt. Describes the causes and effects of inflation. Written with Hazlitt's usual clarity. Distributed by http://mises.org. For ages 16 and up.

MONEYCHANGERS, THE, by Arthur Hailey. A novel about counterfeiting, money and banking. Published by Dell. Out of print. For ages 16 and up.

PLANNED CHAOS by Ludwig von Mises. Compares socialism, fascism, communism, and welfare statism. Mises is one of the greatest. Published by the Foundation for Economic Education, Irvington-on-Hudson, NY 10533. For ages 16 and up.

REASON. Many excellent articles on economics. http://reason.com. For ages 15 and up.

"SAD SAGA OF DIOCLETIAN, THE" by William H. Peterson, *Wall Street Journal*. October 2, 1973, p. 20. Inflation and wage/price controls in the Roman Empire. Excellent history. For ages 16 and up.

UNCLE ERIC BOOKS by Richard J. Maybury. Collectively called *Uncle Eric's Model of the How the World Works*, and includes: 1) UNCLE ERIC TALKS ABOUT PERSONAL, CAREER, AND FINANCIAL SECURITY 2) WHATEVER HAPPENED TO PENNY CANDY? 3) WHATEVER HAPPENED TO JUSTICE? 4) ARE YOU LIBERAL? CONSERVATIVE? OR CONFUSED? 5) ANCIENT ROME: HOW IT AFFECTS YOU TODAY 6) EVALUATING BOOKS: WHAT WOULD THOMAS JEFFERSON THINK ABOUT THIS? 7) THE MONEY MYSTERY (first sequel to PENNY CANDY) 8) THE CLIPPER SHIP STRATEGY (second sequel to PENNY CANDY) 9) THE THOUSAND YEAR WAR IN THE MIDEAST: HOW IT AFFECTS YOU TODAY 10) WORLD WAR I: THE REST OF THE STORY AND HOW IT AFFECTS YOU TODAY 11) WORLD WAR II: THE REST OF THE STORY AND HOW IT AFFECTS YOU TODAY. All published by Bluestocking Press, phone: 800-959-8586, web site: www.BluestockingPress.com. For ages

13 through adult. (Study guides are available for most of the Uncle Eric books.)

WHAT HAS GOVERNMENT DONE TO OUR MONEY? by Murray Rothbard. Distributed by Ludwig Von Mises Institute. An excellent follow up to WHATEVER HAPPENED TO PENNY CANDY. http://mises.org.

YOUNG ENTREPRENEUR'S GUIDE TO STARTING AND RUNNING A BUSINESS, THE, by Steve Mariotti. Includes stories of successful entrepreneurs, business suggestions, philosophy behind entrepreneurship, basic knowledge to run a business successfully, and the nuts-and-bolts of start-up. Published by Times Business, New York. For ages 14 and up.

YOUNG INVESTOR, THE, by Katherine R. Bateman. Explains the language and the craft of investing so that children can grow up business-literate and get an early start at making their money grow. Brief, fun activities teach how to balance a checkbook, read stock tables, and understand terms such as inflation, recession, the Fed, not to mention how to buy and sell savings bonds, mutual funds, and more. Published by Chicago Review Press, Chicago, IL. Ages 10 and up.

# Glossary

*The meaning of economic terms varies according to the viewpoint of the person using them. This glossary contains definitions that the author believes would generally agree with the Austrian school of economics.*

**9-11.** On September 11, 2001, in an attack against the United States, over 3,000 civilians were murdered. The World Trade Center in New York was destroyed as well as a portion of the Pentagon. Four civilian airliners were destroyed, including passengers and crew. This attack is also referred to as Sept. 11 and Sept. 11 Attack.

**BANKNOTE.** Today, paper money. Originally, an IOU from a bank, usually for gold or silver.

**BASE METAL.** A non-precious metal like copper or nickle.

**BLACK MARKET.** Producing, buying, or selling something against the wishes of the government. Example: Liquor was a black market product during the "Prohibition Era."

**BUSINESS.** Production and trade. Also, an organization which produces and/or trades.

**BUSINESS CYCLE.** The boom/bust cycle. Prosperity followed by recession followed by prosperity followed by recession, and so forth.

**CIRCULATION.** The use or trading of money.

**CLAD COIN.** A sandwich coin. A coin made of layers of different metals.

**CLIPPING COINS.** Shaving the edges of a coin in order to get some of the precious metal from the coin.

**COIN.** A wafer or disk of precious metal. True coins usually have three markings; weight, fineness, and name of mint.

**CONSUMER PRICE INDEX (CPI).** The Consumer Price Index (CPI) is the federal government's attempt to measure changes in the prices of items purchased by households. Examples are the prices of automobiles, corn flakes, televisions, haircuts, and lightbulbs. Among the items not included in the CPI are those purchased by governments or by businesses. For instance, large "main frame" computers, airliners, ships, roads, copper ingots, bushels of wheat, and barrels of oil.

**COUNTERFEIT.** Fake, phony.

**CURRENCY.** Money.

**DEBASING.** Reducing the value of a coin by reducing the amount of precious metal in it.

**DEFICIT.** The shortfall between the government's income (taxes) versus its spending. The shortfall is covered either through borrowing or printing money.

**DEFLATION.** A decrease in the amount of money. Usually causes depression and falling prices.

**DEMAND FOR MONEY.** The desire to hold money rather than trade it away. High demand for money means money is traded away reluctantly. Low demand for money means money is traded away quickly.

**DENARIUS.** A Roman coin originally made of 94 percent silver.

**DEPRESSION.** The correction period following an inflation. Usually includes a lot of business failures and unemployment.

**DOUBLE-DIGIT INFLATION.** Price increases rising at 10 to 99 percent per year due to inflation.

**ECONOMICS.** The study of the production and distribution of wealth.

**ECONOMIST.** A person who studies the production and distribution of wealth.

**EXCHANGE.** Trade.

**FEDERAL DEBT.** Total of all Federal deficits.

**FEDERAL RESERVE NOTE.** A slip of paper issued by the U.S. government, used as money, backed by a legal tender law.

**FIAT MONEY.** Legal tender money.

**FINE, FINENESS.** Purity of a precious metal. For instance, if a coin is 900 fine gold, then it is 90 percent gold.

**GRESHAM'S LAW.** A law of economics; says bad money drives good money out of circulation. People hoard good money and trade with legally overvalued money.

**HALLMARK.** The mint-mark of a coin. Tells who made the coin. Like a trademark.

**HARD MONEY.** Non-inflated money, usually a commodity money such as gold or silver.

**INFLATION.** An increase in the amount of money. Causes the money to lose value, so prices rise.

**LAW OF ECONOMICS.** A fact of life which deals with production and distribution of wealth. You cannot change it, and it applies all over the world.

**LAW OF SUPPLY AND DEMAND.** Says that when the supply of something goes up, the price per unit of that thing goes down. When the supply goes down the price goes up.

**LEGAL TENDER LAW.** A law which provides for the punishment of anyone who refuses to accept the legal tender money.

**LEGAL TENDER MONEY.** A legal medium of payment.

**MALINVESTMENT.** Production facilities (land, tools, buildings, or other equipment used to make goods or services) of the wrong type or in the wrong location. Also, stocks, bonds, or other financial assets that have unwarranted demand and exorbitantly high prices.

**MINT.** A factory which makes coins or other money. To make coins out of metal.

**MONEY.** The most easily traded thing in a society. Economists call it the most liquid commodity.

**MONEY DEMAND.** See Demand for Money.

**MONEY SUPPLY.** The amount of money in a country or economy. In recent years economists have begun to try to measure the total world money supply as well as the money supplies of individual countries.

**NATIONAL DEBT.** National debt is federal debt.

**PRECIOUS METAL.** A valuable metal like silver, gold, or platinum.

**PRICE.** What a person wants in trade for what he has.

**PUBLIC WORKS.** Government construction projects, like roads, dams, bridges.

**RECESSION.** The beginning of a depression that never went all the way.

**REEDING.** The notches on the edge of a coin.

**REVOLUTION.** Overthrowing a government, usually by force.

**RUNAWAY INFLATION.** A hyperinflation. Prices rising rapidly, every few hours.

**SOCIALISM.** An economic and political system under which virtually everything and everyone is owned and controlled by government agencies. Marxism.

**SOFT MONEY.** Inflated money. Usually legal tender.

**STAGFLATION.** A combination of too much unemployment and too much inflation, both occurring at the same time.

**SUBSIDY.** A government program for giving tax money away, usually to rich people or large companies. Welfare.

**SUPPLY OF MONEY.** See Money Supply.

**TANSTAAFL.** (Sounds like tans-t-awful) "There Ain't No Such Thing As A Free Lunch." A popular expression during the Great Depression. Means that almost nothing is free, someone must pay for it. TANSTAAFL is a law of economics.

**TAX.** The way governments get money. To tax means to take money away from someone, by force if necessary, even if he thinks what he is getting in return has little or no value.

**TOKEN.** A disk of base metal which can be used as a substitute for a coin.

**VELOCITY.** The speed at which money changes hands.

**WAGE.** The money a person gets for his work.

**WEALTH.** The goods and services people produce or convert to their use.

**WELFARE.** A government program for giving away money or goods, usually to poor people. A subsidy.

**WITHDRAWALS.** The painful process of getting unhooked. Example: a depression is the withdrawal from inflation.

# Index

**Symbols**

9-11, 89

**A**

Adams, John Quincy, 14
American Revolution & tax revolt, 24
America's Founders, 12
America's legal system
  corruption of, 38
Athens, 97
Austrian school of economics, 15, 17
Aztec gold, 50

**B**

banknote, (defined, 34)
banks, 34, 40
base metal, (defined, 20), 26
Belarus, 104
bezant, 98
black market, (defined, 47), 48-49, 91
boom-and-bust cycle, 97
  and 1929 Stock Market Crash, 72
Browne, Harry, 40
Buchanan, James M., 16
business, 15, 19
business cycle, (defined, 55),
  56, 74, 97
Business Cycle Management, 74
Byzantine Empire, 98

**C**

Chicago school of economics, 16
circulation, (defined, 26)
civil law, 102, 103, 105
civil law system, 106
Civil War, inflation, 22
clad coins, (defined, 20)
clipping, (defined, 24)

coin, (defined, 33), 20
  base-metal, 25
  clad, 26
  clipped, 25, 98
  precious-metal, 25
  prior to 1965, 26
  reeded, 26
  shortage, 1960s, 27
Colonial law, 109
common law, 103, 106
Comparison of Law chart, 125
Confederate dollar, 22, 37
Consumer Price Index, 67, 68, 131
Continental dollars, 36, 37
counterfeiting, (defined, 24),
  26, 27, 131
CPI, 131, 132
currency, 63, 134

**D**

daler, 33
Dark Ages, 90
DC-3, 85
debased, 26
debasement, 28
debasing, (defined, 26)
debasing money, 97
debt, federal, 80
Declaration of Independence, 101
deficit, 81, 83
deflation, (defined, 56)
demand for money, 59, 61-63, 66
democracies and inflation, 39
denarius, (defined, 24), 26, 28, 29
depression, (defined, 55), 57, 88, 97-
  99
Destitutionville, 69, 70, 71
Deutschmark, 92
dictatorship, 104
  and inflation, 39
dollar, 31, 32, 33

dollar bill, 20
double-digit inflation, (defined, 22)

**E**

economic feasibility, 85, 86
economic history, 73
economic prosperity, 100, 105, 108
economics, 15, 17, 38, 99, 105
economics, socialist, 103
economist, 59
elections and inflation, 39
English common law, 101, 106
Erhard, Ludwig, 92, 93
ethics, 87, 104
European law, 109
Europe's Dark Ages, 88
exchange, 33

**F**

federal debt, 77, 78, 80, 81
Federal Reserve, 40, 79
Federal Reserve Dollar, 37
Federal Reserve Notes, 20, 34, 35, 36
fiat money, (defined, 35)
fine silver, (defined, 20)
Foundation for Economic Education, 99
Founders, America's, 12
free markets, 12, 101-102, 104-105
French Franc, 34
Friedman, Milton, 16

**G**

German Miracle, 91, 93
Germany, 90-93
glossary, 16
gold, 32, 37, 88, 134, 135, 138
Gold Certificate Dollar, 37
gold coins, circulation of, 37
gold discovery, Australia, 50
gold discovery, California, 50
gold shekel of Babylon, 34
government law, 12, 102, 103
governments and inflation, 39

grape fields of California, 46
Great Depression, 66, 75, 89, 95, 97, 102
and tanstaafl, 23
Greeks, 22
Greenspan, Alan, 15
Gresham's Law, (defined, 26)
grooves, 20

**H**

hallmark, (defined, 33)
hard money, 92
Hayek, Friedrich A., 16
Heritage Foundation, the, 107, 109
Higher Law, 101, 103
Hitler, Adolf, 98
Holland and tulips, 73
Hong Kong, 106
HOW YOU CAN PROFIT FROM THE COMING DEVALUATION, 40

**I**

Inca gold, 50
Index of Economic Freedom, 107-109
individual liberty, 100
inflation, 19-21, (defined, 29) 30, 37, 41, 44, 47, 51, 54, 57, 67-70, 72, 79, 87, 88, 90, 92, 96-99, 131-133, 136, 138
and democracies, 39
and dictatorships, 39
and ethics, 41
and government, 45
runaway, (defined 51) 96
international neutrality, 12
investment decisions, 100
Islamic law, 109

**J**

Joachimthaler, 33
Juris Naturalism, 12

**K**

Kublai Khan, 35

**L**

L, 134
law, 38, 100
   government, 12
   natural, 12
   of economics, (defined, 23)
   of supply and demand, (defined, 28),
      46, 61, 70
"Law Of The Market, the", 105
legal system, 105, 106, 108
legal tender, 20
legal tender law, (defined, 35), 64
   and Kubla Khan, 36
   and South Vietnam, 65
   and the French government, 36
   and the Revolutionary War, 36
legal tender money, 35
legal tender statement, 34, 35
liberty, 12, 101, 102, 105, 108
Lindbergh, Charles, 85, 86

**M**

M1, 134
M2, 76, 134
M3, 134
Magna Carta, 102
malinvestment, 56, 94
Medicare Part D, 104
mint coins, 24
Monetarist school of economics, 15-17
monetary base, 134
money, 15, 20, (defined, 32),
      75, 88, 90, 134
   and law of supply and demand, 28
money supply, 50, (defined, 61), 75,
      79, 89, 95, 131, 133, 135
   inflating, 89
Montgomery Ward, 94
MZM, 134

**N**

national debt, 77, 81
Natural Law, 12, 101-103, 105-106

neutrality, international, 12
New Deal, 97

**O**

oil, 133

**P-Q**

paper money, 35
paradigm shift, 104
piaster, 65
political law, 125
precious metal, (defined, 20)
price controls and World War II, 48
price, 25
price level, 133
printing press and counterfeiting, 24
public works, (defined, 23)

**R**

real estate, 89
real wages, 136
recession/s, 19,-21, (defined, 55), 57,
      66, 75-76, 88-89, 95, 99, 104
   of 1970, 55
   of 1975, 55
   of 1980, 66
   of 1982, 55, 66, 75
   of 2001, 79
   post WWII, 95
reeded, (defined, 25)
reeding, 20
revolutions, 39
rising price/s, 30, 71
risk, 105, 108
Roaring '90s, 67, 68, 79
Roaring Twenties, 65, 67
Roman Empire, 15, 29, 90, 103
   and inflation, 22
   government, 23, 24, 27
   Law, 102, 104-106
   Republic, 103
Roosevelt, Franklin, 97

runaway inflation, (defined, 51), 53,
  63, 96, 98
  Chile 1970s, 63
  Germany, 51
  Hungary, 51
  American, 63

**S**

savings, 82, 83
scientific law, 125
Sears, 94
silver, 32, 37, 88, 134, 135, 138
Silver Certificate, 20, 34
Silver Certificate Dollar, 37
silver coins, circulation of, 37
silver shekel, 34
Simon, Treasury Secretary William,
  83
slavery, 102
social security, 136
socialism, 103, 104
socialist law, 104
Spanish conquistadors, 50
specialization of labor, 90
stages of inflation, 62
statism, 104
stock market, 79
Stock Market Crash of 1929, 68, 72
stock market crash of 1987, 76
stocks, 67, 75, 132
strike, 47
subsidy, (defined, 23)
supply and demand, law of, 131
supply of money, 29, 64, 66, 72
  decreases in, 49
  increases in, 49
  inflating, 29
Switzerland, 50, 90

**T**

TANSTAAFL, (defined, 23), 41, 46,
  90, 99
tax/es, 27, 83, 84, 92, 105, 132
  income, 80

Taxing, (defined, 24)
thaler, 33, 90
Tianamen Square, 104
tokens, (defined, 20)
tools, 82, 83
tulipmania, 73, 89
two fundamental laws, 101-102, 104-
  105, 108

**U**

U.S. Constitution, Article One,
  Section Ten, 36
unemployment, 87-88
Union of Soviet Socialist Republics
  (USSR), 103
unions, 45, 49

**V**

Valley Forge, 37
velocity, (defined, 59), 60-64, 66,
  96, 133
Venezuela, 104

**W-Z**

wage/price controls, 43, 46-47, 49-
  50, 91-92
  and the Roman government, 47
wage/price spiral, 41, 43-44, 49-
  50, 87
wages, 43, 84
  and prices, fall in, 49
  and prices, increases in, 49
*Wall Street Journal*, 107, 109
Washington, George, 37
wealth, 80
welfare program, (defined, 23)
withdrawals, 57
World War I, 102
World War II, 94
  and price controls, 48
  and the black market, 48
Wright Brothers, 85

# About Richard J. Maybury

President of Henry Madison Research, Inc., Richard Maybury, also known as Uncle Eric, is a world renowned author, lecturer, and geopolitical analyst. He consults with business firms in the U.S. and Europe. Mr. Maybury is the former Global Affairs editor of MONEYWORLD and widely regarded as one of the finest free-market writers in America. His articles have appeared in THE WALL STREET JOURNAL, USA TODAY, and other major publications.

Richard Maybury has penned eleven books in the Uncle Eric series. His books have been endorsed by top business leaders including former U.S. Treasury Secretary William Simon, and he has been interviewed on more than 250 radio and TV shows across America.

He has been married for more than 42 years, has lived abroad, traveled around the world, and visited 48 states and 45 countries.

He is truly a teacher for all ages.

# Published by Bluestocking Press

## Uncle Eric Books by Richard J. Maybury

UNCLE ERIC TALKS ABOUT PERSONAL, CAREER, AND FINANCIAL SECURITY

WHATEVER HAPPENED TO PENNY CANDY?

WHATEVER HAPPENED TO JUSTICE?

ARE YOU LIBERAL? CONSERVATIVE? OR CONFUSED?

ANCIENT ROME: HOW IT AFFECTS YOU TODAY

EVALUATING BOOKS: WHAT WOULD THOMAS JEFFERSON THINK ABOUT THIS?

THE MONEY MYSTERY

THE CLIPPER SHIP STRATEGY

THE THOUSAND YEAR WAR IN THE MIDEAST

WORLD WAR I: THE REST OF THE STORY

WORLD WAR II: THE REST OF THE STORY

**Bluestocking Guides (student study guides for selected Uncle Eric books)**
by Jane A. Williams and/or Kathryn Daniels

Each student study guide includes some or all of the following:

1) chapter-by-chapter comprehension questions and answers
2) application questions and answers
3) research activities
4) essay assignments
5) thought questions
6) final exam

**More Bluestocking Press Titles**

CAPITALISM FOR KIDS: GROWING UP TO BE YOUR OWN BOSS by Karl Hess

COMMON SENSE BUSINESS FOR KIDS by Kathryn Daniels

ECONOMICS: A FREE MARKET READER edited by Jane Williams & Kathryn Daniels

## Order information

Order any of the above by phone or online from:

### Bluestocking Press

Phone: 800-959-8586

email: CustomerService@BluestockingPress.com

web site: www.BluestockingPress.com